Great Myths and Legends

Great Myths and Legends

The 1984 Childcraft Annual

An annual supplement to
Childcraft—The How and Why Library

World Book, Inc.

a Scott Fetzer company

Chicago London Sydney Toronto

Copyright © 1984
World Book, Inc.
Merchandise Mart Plaza, Chicago, Illinois 60654
All rights reserved
Printed in the United States of America
ISBN 0-7166-0684-4
Library of Congress Catalog Card No. 65-25105

Acknowledgments

Houghton Mifflin Company: "A Song of Greatness"
from *The Children Sing in the Far West* by Mary
Austin, copyright 1928 by Mary Austin. Copyright ©
renewed 1956 by Kenneth M. Chapman and Mary C.
Wheelwright. Reprinted by permission of Houghton
Mifflin Company.

Contents

7 Preface

9 The Dragon Slayer

21 The Sea Monster

33 The Terrible Lion-Man

45 The Dreadful Guest

51 The Captive Princess

73 The Saving of Tam Lin

83 The Journey to Find the Sun

105 The Creature in the Forest

117 The Island of the Ogres

129 Finn and the Goblin

149 The Changing of the Sea People

161 The Prince and the Evil Sorcerer

176 The Brave Coward

191 The Monster in the Maze

205 The Green Knight's Challenge

219 The Evil Old Witch

237 The City Without a King

249 The Many-Headed Monster

257 The Quest for the Sampo

281 The Wicked Enchantment

292 A Short Dictionary of Myth and Legend

304 Illustration Acknowledgments

Preface

Myths and legends are stories that have come down to us from the distant past. As you will discover, these are exciting tales of adventure, filled with sorcerers and witches, dragons and goblins, and all kinds of magic. Each is a story of good against evil.

All of these tales were told by storytellers long before they were written down. And they were told with a purpose. Myths are about gods and goddesses and superhuman beings. They were generally told to explain a belief or something in nature. Legends are almost always based on something that actually happened. They were told to glorify someone who had performed great deeds or caused marvelous things to happen.

But most of all, these are tales of heroes and heroines, young and old. They have the qualities their people most admired—courage, wisdom, goodness, strength, self-sacrifice, gentleness, loyalty, generosity, honesty, and kindness. And, like the Indian boy in the following song, when their time came, they did what was expected of them.

A Song of Greatness

A Chippewa Indian song
Transcribed by Mary Austin

When I hear the old men
Telling of heroes,
Telling of great deeds
Of ancient days,
When I hear them telling,
Then I think within me
I too am one of these.

When I hear the people
Praising great ones,
Then I know that I too
Shall be esteemed,
I too when my time comes
Shall do mightily.

The Dragon Slayer

This story comes from a poem that is considered the first great work of English literature. The poem was written in England more than twelve hundred years ago, but the action takes place in Denmark and Sweden. It is the story of the adventures of a mighty warrior named Beowulf (BAY uh wulf). He has all the qualities most admired by the Anglo-Saxon people who lived in England at that time—strength, courage, loyalty, and generosity. As in many legends, this is the story of a man who sets out to do his duty, even though he knows it will cost him his life.

The Dragon Slayer

ong, long ago, in a wild and lonely part of
the land now called Sweden, there lived an old man. He
lived alone, in an old building that stood at the foot of a
hill. He was the last of the family of chiefs and warriors
that had ruled the countryside for hundreds of years.
The old building had been their hall. Now, it was
half-ruined and falling apart.

But the ancient hall was filled with the riches the
man's ancestors had won in many battles. Swords with
jeweled hilts hung on the walls. Chests of gold and
silver rings, brooches, and bracelets were piled in the
corners. Upon the tables sat goblets, bowls, and plates
of gold, decorated with jewels.

One autumn day, the first wind of winter was blowing
out of the north. The old man knew he was coming to
the end of his days. His life would soon be done. He
looked about at the gleam of gold and silver, and the
wink and sparkle of jewels.

"I must not leave these things for strangers to have,"
he said to himself. "They were won by the might and

blood of my ancestors! I will hide them forever from the light of day!"

He trudged to the top of the hill. Here, there arose a great mound of grass-covered earth. At the foot of this mound was a pile of rocks. The old man removed the rocks to reveal a large opening in the mound. Within, was a great room, with walls made of stones. In the room lay the bones of many of the old man's ancestors. This was their burial mound.

Day after day, a little at a time, the man brought loads of treasure from the hall to the hilltop. He put the treasure in a great pile inside the room.

Finally, the task was nearly done. The man intended to return the next day and cover up the hole once more. The treasure would be hidden forever.

But, when the next day dawned, the old man did not awaken. His days were done. He had died in his sleep. The entrance to the burial mound remained uncovered.

Many a winter and summer came and went. The old hall crumbled away into a pile of wood and stone. The entrance to the burial mound stayed open, like a yawning mouth on the hilltop.

At that time, dragons still lived upon the earth. And one day, a dragon came flying out of the far north. It was seeking a cave in which to make its den. Its keen eyes spied the hole on the hilltop.

The dragon came circling down to land near the entrance to the mound. It entered the chamber, dimly lit with daylight that shone through the entrance. At the sight of the pile of treasure, the dragon's red eyes lit up with delight. For dragons love gold, jewels, and precious things even more than do people.

The dragon made the cave and treasure his own. By
day, he lay slumbering upon the gleaming and glittering
pile. He would awaken, at times, to lovingly lick and
sniff at the precious metals and jewels. By night, he
hunted among the hills, for deer and other creatures to
feed his hunger.

Long of life are dragons. For three hundred years did
the great scaled beast guard the treasure. In all that
time, no man came near the dragon's hilltop home.

Then, late one night, a man did come. He was a
criminal, fleeing those who wished to see him punished
for his crimes. It was a stormy, windy night, and the
man sought shelter. He chanced to see the opening in
the mound and quickly went within.

He kindled a small fire to dry his dripping garments. In amazement, he stared at the sight of the treasure, gleaming in the fire's glow. But he also saw the marks the dragon's claws had left upon the floor. He knew he stood in a dragon's den. Snatching up a gold, bejeweled cup, he fled in fear, back out into the stormy darkness.

At sunrise, the dragon returned to his den. At once, he saw the signs and smelled the scent that told him a human had entered his home. And, with rising rage he saw that the cup was missing, for he knew every piece of his treasure!

He rushed forth from the den, spread wide his wings, and sprang into the air. Circling in and out among the hills, he searched for the thief. But the man was now far away. In time, the dragon returned to the hilltop. His eyes burning red with rage, he pondered how to gain revenge for the loss of a part of his treasure.

Far beyond the hills lay a plain. And there, the dragon knew, were many villages and farms. He would punish the people who lived in those places for the loss of his cup! Once again, he sprang into the air and went winging on his way.

In a village just beyond the hills, people were just awaking in the morning light. The dragon came upon them like a flash of lightning. In frightful fury, he swooped over the rooftops, spitting streams of fire that set rows of houses ablaze. Back and forth over the village he sped, spreading trails of flame.

When the dragon finally turned from its fiery task and headed for home, the whole village was in flames. The weeping and wailing of the people filled the air.

That night, the dragon attacked another town and burnt it to the ground. The following day, he destroyed a number of farms. The fields of golden grain were turned into smoking ashes.

Terror spread through the plains. A group of people journeyed to the hall of their king to ask his help. "The smoke of burning rises across the land, O King," they told him. "Soon, there will not be a building standing upon the plain. Your people ask you to save us from this terror!"

The king's name was Beowulf. For fifty years he had ruled the land of the Geats. He was an old man, with hair and beard the color of winter's snow. But in his youth he had been a mighty warrior who feared nothing. His eyes were still blue and fierce, and his shoulders were broad.

Beowulf looked about at his young warriors. They looked away. He knew they were afraid he might ask one of them to fight the fire-breathing dragon. He laughed at them, scornfully.

"My days are nearly done," he told the people who had come to ask for help. "But it is better to die battling for my people than to die in bed, an old, weak man! I will go against the dragon!"

He had a great shield of iron made for himself, for he knew a wooden shield would be useless against the dragon's fire. Then he picked out twelve of his sturdiest warriors, and set out for the dragon's hilltop.

It was a gray, sunless day when they reached the hill. Wisps of fog crept around their feet. Dark smoke hung over the mound in which the dragon lay slumbering. Beowulf and his warriors plodded toward it.

But halfway up the hill, the king ordered his men to halt. "Stand here until I have need of you," he told them. Then he went on, alone.

When he reached the mound, he peered into the entrance. In the dim light and the haze of smoke he could see the huge form of the dragon, asleep on the pile of treasure.

"Dragon," he called in a loud voice, "I am Beowulf, king of the Geats. I challenge you to come forth and do battle with me!"

The dragon's eyes flashed open. He hissed in anger. With footsteps that shook the earth, he came forth from the mound. Thrusting his head forward, he breathed out a fierce blast of fire. Beowulf crouched behind his metal shield. The fire beat against it, throwing great spurts of flame into the air. Some of these fell toward the cluster of warriors, and they turned and fled in fear!

When the dragon's breath of flame came to an end, Beowulf stepped forward and swung his sword with all his strength. The blade bit deep into the dragon's neck! The creature's roar of rage was horrible to hear! Again, it sent a long, terrible blast of fire against the old king. The flame spread around the edges of the shield, singeing Beowulf's beard and scorching his clothes. He staggered back, faint from the frightful heat.

Wiglaf, youngest of the king's warriors, was ashamed

to see the old man facing the dragon alone. He rushed up the hill. The dragon turned to face this new enemy, and Beowulf saw his chance. Again, he struck with all his might. But this time, his sword shattered against the monster's thick scales.

The dragon shrieked in pain and fury. It lunged at the old king, knocking him to the ground. It sank its poisonous, dagger-sharp teeth into his shoulder.

With teeth gritted, Wiglaf thrust his spear deep into the dragon's scaly body. The beast shuddered and lifted its head. At once, Beowulf snatched the dagger from his belt, and plunged it into the dragon's throat.

It was the deathblow for the dragon. The light of life faded from its eyes. Lifeless, it lay sprawled across Beowulf's body.

But Beowulf, too, was breathing his last. His shoulder was swollen with the dragon's foul poison. Weakly, he whispered his last words to Wiglaf.

"Use the treasure to help the people rebuild their homes and farms," he told the young man. "And to you, who alone of all my warriors came to aid me, I leave my kingdom. You are now the king of the Geats."

Then his eyes closed and he breathed no more.

Sadly and in shame, the other warriors gathered around him. They made a stretcher out of tree branches, and on it carried Beowulf home to his hall. On a cliff by the sea, a great burial mound was made. Within it, the body of Beowulf was laid to rest.

After a few summers, the burial mound was green with the cover of grass. But, for many long years, the Geats remembered Beowulf. When younger men had held back in fear, the old king had given his life to slay the dragon and save his people.

The Sea Monster

This tale of a sea monster, a girl named Andromeda, and a man named Perseus, comes from ancient Greece. It is thousands of years old. It is a typical Greek myth, in which an angry god causes great trouble for people, but a brave hero makes everything right.

The Sea Monster

Long ago, at the edge of the sparkling
Mediterranean Sea there stood a great city known as
Joppa. It was ruled by a king named Cepheus. He and
his wife, Queen Cassiopeia, had a daughter named
Andromeda, who was the most beautiful young woman
in all Joppa—and perhaps in all the lands that
surrounded Joppa, as well.

Cassiopeia was immensely proud of her daughter's
beauty. One day, as she watched Andromeda walk along
the seashore, she said in a loud voice, "Ah, how
fortunate I am to have such a beautiful daughter.
Andromeda is more beautiful than even the Nereids!"

Now, the Nereids were mermaids. They were known
far and wide for their great beauty, and were very proud
of themselves. Alas, as luck would have it, they were
swimming in the sea nearby, and they heard
Cassiopeia's words.

Furious, they swam to Poseidon, the god of the sea.
"Great Poseidon, we have been insulted," they raged.
"Cassiopeia, the Queen of Joppa, has said that her

daughter is more beautiful than we! She must be
punished!"

Nothing made a god more angry than to learn that a
mortal had not shown enough respect for him or his
followers. "She shall be punished," roared Poseidon, in a
voice like waves smashing against rocks. "And her
daughter's beauty shall be removed from the world!"

The next morning, the fishermen of Joppa went out
upon the sea in their boats as they always did. But
suddenly, a huge and horrible monster rose up out of
the sparkling water! Seven times taller than a tall man
it was, and covered with thick scales. Its huge mouth
was filled with sharp, pointed teeth, and on its hands
were long, curved claws. It began to smash boats and
devour men! Only a few fishermen managed to turn
back and get safely to shore.

The monster then waded out of the water and onto

the land. It began to destroy the farmlands all around the city. It trampled the fields of grain, and devoured the herds of sheep.

As days passed, the people of Joppa began to suffer badly. They had no fish to eat, because the fishermen dared not go out upon the sea. They had no bread, for there was no grain from which to make it. They had no cheese, butter, milk, or meat, because the herds of sheep were gone. And no ships dared bring food to the city, because the monster would destroy them.

Huge crowds of wailing people filled the street in front of King Cepheus' palace. "We are starving!" they cried. "You must do something!"

King Cepheus felt there must be some way to get rid of the dreadful monster. He called upon his wise men to find out why the monster had come, and how it could be driven away.

The wise men burned magical powders and studied the swirling smoke. They gazed at the patterns of the stars. After a time, they returned to the king and told him what they had learned.

"This sea monster was sent by the god Poseidon," they told Cepheus. "It is a punishment because Queen Cassiopeia said that Andromeda is more beautiful than Poseidon's loved ones, the Nereids. The only way you can get rid of the monster is by sacrificing your daughter to it! She must be chained to a rock by the sea so that the monster may devour her. Otherwise, your people will starve to death and the city of Joppa will become an empty ruin!"

This was the god Poseidon's vengeance. He would punish Cassiopeia, as he had promised, by making her the cause of her daughter's death. And he would remove

Andromeda's beauty from the world, as he had said, by
letting the monster eat her!

Cepheus groaned with grief when he heard this news,
and Cassiopeia wept. "We cannot let Andromeda be a
sacrifice," they cried.

Andromeda had turned pale. But she said, "If this is the only way that the people and the city can be saved, I must do it."

And so, a few days later, Andromeda let herself be chained to a tall rock near the edge of the sea. Her weeping parents stood nearby. They wished to be with her as long as they could, before the sea monster arrived to claim its sacrifice.

It was a beautiful day, and Andromeda gazed about at the sparkling sea, the blue sky, and the golden seashore. Her eyes filled with tears at the thought that this would be her last sight of the beauties of the world—for she would soon be dead. But as she gazed up into the sky, she gave a gasp of surprise. A man was flying through the air!

The man had also seen Andromeda. He swooped down and landed on the beach beside her. She saw that he flew by means of magic sandals that had pairs of wings on them. He was a tall, sturdy, handsome young man.

"Maiden," he said, staring at Andromeda, "who are you? Why are you chained to this rock?"

"My name is Andromeda," she told him. "I am the daughter of King Cepheus and Queen Cassiopeia. I am to be sacrificed this day to a sea monster that has attacked my father's kingdom."

The young man saw that Andromeda was very frightened, but was doing her best not to cry. He thought she was extremely brave. He also thought she was the most beautiful girl he had ever seen.

"I shall set you free!" he exclaimed, grasping her chains. "I can carry you off to where this monster cannot find you."

But Andromeda sadly shook her head. "You must not," she told him. "Unless I am sacrificed, the monster will destroy my father's kingdom. Only if I let it eat me, will it leave our kingdom and our people in peace."

The man was more impressed than ever by Andromeda's courage. She was going to let herself be eaten in order to save her land and people! He turned toward Cepheus and Cassiopeia, whom he had guessed to be Andromeda's parents.

"Hear my words, king and queen of Joppa," he said. "I am Perseus, son of Zeus, who is king of all the gods. I am the conqueror of the dreaded monster Medusa who was so hideous that any living thing that saw her turned to stone! I do not fear this sea monster that threatens your kingdom. If I can kill it, and save Andromeda, will you agree to let her marry me, if she is willing to do so?"

"Indeed, we gladly agree," they cried.

Perseus turned back to Andromeda. "I will fight this creature for you," he said, gently. "If I can kill it, and save you and your father's kingdom, will you become my wife?"

Andromeda looked at him for a moment. She decided that he must truly love her if he was willing to risk his life against the dreadful sea monster in order to save her. If he loved her that much, he would be a good husband, she felt.

"I will marry you, Perseus," she told him.

At that moment, the sea monster rose up out of the water. With an earsplitting hiss, it began to wade in toward the beach.

Perseus drew his sword and leaped into the air. The wings on his sandals began to flap, and he flew straight

at the monster's head. He struck a blow that sliced into its neck. The creature hissed with rage, and slashed at Perseus with its terrible claws. But Perseus dodged aside.

Around and around the monster's head Perseus darted and dodged. Again and again he cut the creature, until it was covered with wounds. Soon it grew weak from loss of blood and began to move more slowly. Finally, Perseus was able to fly in close. With a mighty blow, he cut off the monster's head.

Thus was Andromeda and the city of Joppa saved from the dreadful sea monster. And thus did Perseus gain a brave and beautiful wife.

The Terrible Lion-Man

Long ago, the Malinke people were part of the great
Mali Empire in western Africa. Today, they live in
what is now the nation of Mali. This tale is part of a
long song that the Malinke still sing.

The song is sometimes sung at special ceremonies
for hunters—for the hero of the story, Kambili, is a
hunter. The song tells how Kambili and his wife,
Kumba, risk their lives to protect people who have
come to them for help. It is obvious that the
Malinke have great respect for men and women who
try to help others.

The Terrible Lion-Man

here was fear throughout the land of the
Malinke people. When the sun set and the red sky
turned black, people huddled in terror in their huts. For
in the night a lion-man prowled the land—a man who at
night took the form of a lion! In the darkness he would
steal silently into a village, to kill and devour the
people!

Messengers were sent from many of the villages. All
headed in the same direction—across the plain to the
village where the great warrior Kambili dwelt. To
Kambili's hut, each messenger went. They all brought
the same message. "Kambili, great warrior, help us!
Search out this terrible lion-man and kill him before
more of our people are killed. Only you can do this!"

To each man, Kambili gave the same answer. "It shall
be done."

But before he could slay the evil lion-man, Kambili
had to find out who the lion-man was. This called for
magic. Kambili's wife, the beautiful Kumba, could make
such magic, for she was a skilled sorceress. Kambili

waited while she cast spells. In the language of magic,
she sang songs that asked questions. She listened as the
voices of unseen spirits whispered answers into her ear.
Then she turned to her husband.

"I have found out who the lion-man is," she said to
Kambili. "But you cannot simply go and slay him. He is
a powerful wizard, and cannot be killed by ordinary
means. It will take great magic to help you slay
him—greater magic than mine."

Kambili pondered for a time. Then he said, "The
greatest of all magicians is Bari, the Truth Seeker. Let
us go ask him what must be done."

Together, they went to the hut of Bari, the Truth
Seeker. He was an old man, with a beard as gray as the
ashes of a wood fire. He listened to the words of Kumba
and Kambili. Then he told them what they must do.

"Somehow, you must get some hair from the
lion-man's head," said Bari. "And you must get a sandal
that he has worn upon his foot. Bury the hair and the

sandal in the earth before the carved idol of Nya-ji. The idol will tell you how to defeat the lion-man."

"But, how can we do this?" wondered Kambili. "I cannot just go and ask the man to give me some hair and a sandal! I cannot creep into his hut like a thief and steal such things."

"I think I know how to get them, husband," said Kumba. "I will go to the man's hut and tell him I have fallen in love with him and want him to marry me. I shall offer to cook his dinner, to show what a good wife I would be. Into his food I will mix the juice of a certain plant. It will make him sleep soundly. When he is asleep, I will cut off a bit of his hair and take one of his sandals. Then I will return to you."

"If he should awaken, you will be in great danger," said Kambili, anxiously. "I do not want you to put yourself in such danger."

"You have often put yourself in danger to do what must be done," said she. "Now, I must put myself in danger, too. There is no other way."

Kambili reached out and put his arms around her. "Very well," he said, sadly.

Kumba journeyed to the village of the evil magician who was the lion-man. She went to his hut and found him sitting outside it.

"I have watched you, although you never saw me," she told the man. "I have come to love you! I know you are a great and powerful man, and I want to be your wife. Let me cook a meal for you, to show you what a fine wife I would make."

Kumba was very beautiful. The man was delighted to think that she wanted to marry him. "Come into my home," he said. "By all means you may cook a meal for me!"

Kumba entered the hut. She prepared a delicious meal for the man. But while the food was cooking, she poured in a small amount of sleeping potion. The man ate the food, praising it, and assuring Kumba that he would marry her. However, he soon began to yawn, and it was not long before he was sound asleep and snoring.

With a knife, Kumba very carefully sliced off a tiny bit of the man's hair. Then she carefully removed one of his sandals. Quickly, she left the hut and hurried back to her village to join Kambili.

"I have what is needed," she cried happily, holding up the sandal and the pinch of hair for him to see.

"That is good. But best of all is that you have come back safely," said Kambili, hugging her.

Together, they went to the idol of Nya-ji. The idol was the figure of a tall man with large, staring eyes. It was carved out of a huge tree trunk. With the blade of his spear, Kambili dug a hole in the earth in front of the idol. He placed the pinch of hair and the sandal in the hole and covered them up with earth.

Suddenly, a deep, booming voice came from the idol. It said, "This man can be slain in only one place in all the world—within the grove of trees that stands on the plain near the village of Jimini. You must make him come to that place. You must await him there, and slay him when he comes." Then the voice was silent.

"I must think of how to make the lion-man come to that grove," said Kambili. "What would make him come?"

"He would come if he thought there was easy food for him there," said Kumba. "When men want to catch a lion, they tie a young goat to a tree and then hide nearby. The lion sees the goat and thinks it is easy prey. But when the lion comes close enough, the men rush out of hiding and slay it. Could we not set such a trap for the lion-man?"

Kambili shook his head. "The evil lion-man would not eat a goat. He wants only human flesh!"

"Then we must bait the trap with a human," said Kumba. "I will be the bait. I will sit in the grove like a little tied-up goat. I will sing a magical song that will make the lion-man come to me. You must hide nearby. When the lion-man comes for me, you can slay him."

"Again you are putting yourself in dreadful danger," cried Kambili. "I do not want you to take such a risk!"

"I will not be in danger with you there to save me," Kumba answered. "*You* are the one who will be in danger, for you must fight a large, savage lion! If you can take such a great risk, I can take a small one."

"I suppose it must be," said Kambili. "But I do not like it."

They walked to the grove near the village of Jimini. It was late afternoon when they started out, and nearly sunset when they arrived. Kumba sat down with her back against a tree. Kambili hid himself in some nearby bushes.

The setting sun tinted the plain red. As the sun slid lower in the sky, the red became purple, and then black.

Overhead, the white moon and the glittering stars appeared. This was the time when the lion-man came out to hunt!

Kumba began to sing. It was a magical song, with words in the language of magic. It told how she was all alone in the grove.

The song drifted across the plain. It was too faint to be heard, but its magic floated through the night. Far out on the plain, the lion-man, now a big, powerful lion, prowled. The song reached him. He did not hear it, but its magic made him think of a tender, tasty girl, all alone in the grove of trees near Jimini. He felt that he must go there. Licking his lips hungrily, he began to trot across the plain.

But the lion-man was a magician, too, and as he ran across the plain he sent a spell ahead of him—a spell of sleep. Kumba was still singing her spell, and so the magic that surrounded her protected her from the magic of the lion-man. But Kambili was unprotected. His eyelids grew heavy, and his head began to nod. Soon, he was in a deep, magical sleep!

After a time, Kumba knew that something had entered the grove. Looking about, she saw the lion, standing in a patch of moonlight between two trees. His big body looked silver in the moonlight, and his glowing green eyes stared at her hungrily.

Kumba stopped singing. "He has come," she called softly to Kambili.

But then, because she had stopped singing, she felt

the power of the lion-man's magic. She suddenly
realized that Kambili had been put to sleep by the spell.
He could not protect her! She was helpless against the
huge lion—and, it was getting ready to attack! Its tail
swung from side to side as the big beast crouched,
making ready to spring.

Quickly, Kumba sang a spell to release Kambili from
the lion-man's magic.

"Kambili, now awaken quickly!
Your spear is needed to defend me!"

Kambili's eyes flashed open. He saw the lion,
crouched to spring. With a shout, he dashed out of his
hiding place and flung himself in front of Kumba. At
that instant, the lion sprang. It hurtled through the air,
its paws outstretched, its terrible claws spread to rip
and slash!

Kambili thrust out his stout spear. The lion's leap
carried it straight onto the razor-sharp point. The point
ripped through the lion's body and into its heart. The
huge beast plunged to the ground, shuddered, and was
still.

A moment later, the lion's body began to change.
Slowly, it turned back into the body of the evil magician
who had brought so much fear to the land of the
Malinke. But now, he lay dead. No longer would the
land be troubled by his wicked magic!

Kambili and Kumba returned to their village. Great
was the rejoicing when they announced that the
lion-man was no more. The people gave great honor to
Kambili for his courage in killing the lion-man. But to
Kumba, they gave even greater honor. For in truth it
was the brave and clever Kumba who had discovered
the way to find and slay the lion-man!

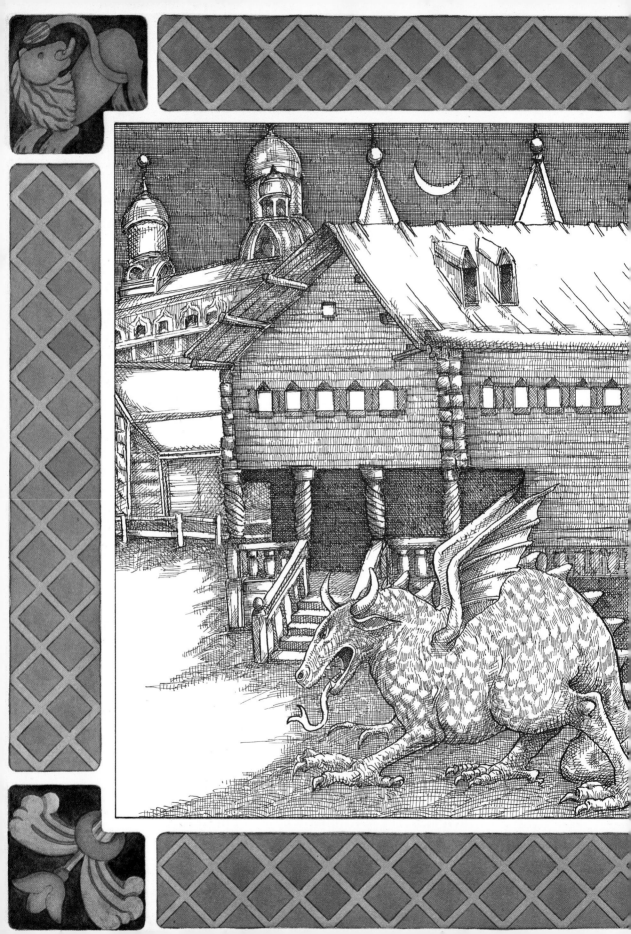

The Dreadful Guest

This story takes place in Russia, about a thousand years ago. It is one of a group of legends called *byliny* (BUH lee nee), meaning "what has been." The tales tell of the adventures of the hero-warriors who belonged to the court of Vladimir I, prince of the city of Kiev.

In the legends of many lands, the heroic warriors are knights, nobles, or even kings. But the warriors of these Russian legends are usually common farmers or merchants. And while the legends of most lands are serious and sometimes sad, the Russian tales are often sly and funny.

The Dreadful Guest

Prince Vladimir of Kiev was giving a great feast. Scores of princes, boyars (nobles), rich merchants, and a hero or two sat at the long table in the feast hall. The room rang with talk and laughter.

Suddenly, a huge, horrible creature came stomping in. It was Tugarin the dragon! He was twice as tall as a man, with teeth like spikes and claws like knives. When he opened his mouth, flames shot forth, and black smoke curled up out of his nostrils. Tugarin walked to the table and pushed himself between Prince Vladimir and his wife, Princess Apraksya!

No one said a word. Everyone was too frightened. Everyone, that is, except the hero Alyosha Popovich. He glared angrily at the monster, and in a loud voice asked, "What kind of ill-mannered creature are you?"

Before Tugarin could reply, servants entered the room carrying a huge roast swan on a platter. They set the platter down in front of Prince Vladimir. But as the prince was about to begin carving the bird, Tugarin snatched it up and swallowed it whole.

"You have no more manners than a pig!" exclaimed Alyosha Popovich. "I hope you choke to death on the bones!"

Tugarin scowled, making all the guests shudder in fear. But Alyosha Popovich simply laughed.

Next, servants brought in a large flagon of wine. They placed the wine in front of Princess Apraksya. But Tugarin seized the flagon and, in an instant, drank every drop of the wine.

"What a glutton!" yelled Alyosha Popovich. "My father once had a cow who was the same way. One day she broke into the cellar and drank so much wine she swelled up and burst! I hope that happens to you, Tugarin Dragon!"

This was too much for the dragon. He sprang to his feet. "Will you come outside and fight me, Alyosha Popovich?" he roared.

"Of course," said the hero, with a cheerful smile.

Tugarin stomped out of the room. Alyosha Popovich got up to follow him.

"Oh, Alyosha," said Princess Apraksya, "why did you challenge him? We could have put up with him until he left. Now you'll be killed!"

Most of the princes, boyars, and rich merchants agreed that Alyosha Popovich had no chance at all against the dragon. They began to make bets among themselves as to how long it would take Tugarin to finish off the hero!

Alyosha walked out into the palace courtyard, where the dragon awaited him. He strolled forward until he was standing right in front of Tugarin. But he didn't draw his sword.

"Well, Alyosha Popovich, how would you like to die?"

asked Tugarin with a dreadful smile. "Shall I chew you
to bits with my spike teeth? Shall I slice you to pieces
with my knife claws? Shall I roast you to a cinder with
my fiery breath?"

But Alyosha put his hands on his hips and scowled.
"Now, see here, Tugarin Dragon," he said angrily, "this
was to be a fight between just the two of us!" He
pointed at something behind the dragon. "Why have
you brought an army here to help you fight?"

Dragons are not very clever, but heroes are. Tugarin
turned his head to see what Alyosha Popovich was
talking about. Quick as a finger snap, Alyosha drew his
sword and cut off the monster's head!

Then he put away his sword and strolled back into
the feast hall. "The fight's over," he announced. "We
won't have to put up with Tugarin's terrible table
manners ever again!"

And, as everyone stood up to cheer, Alyosha
Popovich sat down to eat!

The Captive Princess

This tale of a captive princess is based upon a long and beautiful poem. The poem was written by a poet named Valmiki, in India, more than two thousand years ago. Called the *Ramayana* ("Romance of Rama"), it is probably based on stories that had been told for hundreds of years before they were put into writing.

The *Ramayana* is one of India's greatest and most treasured works of literature. It remains popular today because it is an exciting story filled with magic and adventure and has heroes and a heroine who are courageous and loyal to one another.

The Captive Princess

ich, peaceful, and happy was the kingdom of
Kosala. Wise and good was its king, Dasaratha, who
dwelt in the great city of Ayodhya.

Dasaratha had three wives and four sons. The eldest
son was the brave, handsome, and good Prince Rama.
He was adored and respected throughout the land, and
greatly loved by his father, the king.

A time came when Dasaratha felt he was too old to
rule any longer. He announced that he would make
Rama the ruler of Kosala in his place. The people
rejoiced to hear that Prince Rama would be their new
king.

But, on the very day that Rama was to become king,
Dasaratha's second wife, Kaikeyi, came to him. She was
the mother of his second son, Bharata.

"Lord," said Kaikeyi, "do you remember that long ago
you made me a promise? You promised that anything I
asked for, you would give me."

"I remember," said King Dasaratha.

"Never have I asked for anything until now," she

said. "But now, I ask that you make our son, Bharata, king instead of Rama! I ask that you order Rama to leave this land for fourteen years!"

Dasaratha hung his head and wept. His heart was like a heavy stone, for he knew he would not live to see his son again. But he could not break his promise. He called Rama to him, and told the prince that he would not be king. Weeping, he told Rama that he must leave Kosala.

Rama, too, was crushed with grief. He, too, wept—not because he would not be king, but because he had to leave his father and the land he loved. But he would not disobey his father. He returned to his home and made ready to leave.

His wife, the beautiful Princess Sita, came to him. "Where are you going, my husband?" she asked.

"I must leave Kosala," Rama told her. "I have been sent away for fourteen years. I must go and live in exile in the great forest beyond the river."

"Then I will go with you," said Sita. "For, where you go, I shall go."

"You must not come with me," said Rama, sadly. "Life in the forest would be too hard and dangerous for you. For food, there is only the fruit of trees, and for a bed there is only the ground. Tigers and other wild beasts prowl among the trees and deadly serpents lurk among the bushes! It is a place of darkness, hunger, and fear!"

"That does not matter," she said, smiling at him. "I want to be with you, wherever you are."

He saw that she would not change her mind. And, while he was sad to think of the hardships and danger she would face, he was overjoyed that she would be with him.

As Prince Rama and Princess Sita made ready to leave, Rama's younger brother Prince Lakshmana came to them. He had always been Rama's closest companion. Since boyhood, they had played together, learned their lessons together, and hunted together. Great was their love for one another.

"I am going with you, brother," said Lakshmana with a grin.

And so the three of them set out in Rama's swift chariot. They drove through streets thronged with people who had gathered to sadly call farewell to their beloved prince.

In time, Rama and his wife and brother came to the edge of the great forest. It spread out across the land as far as the eye could see. Through the forest flowed a

river, like a pale blue snake. Rama and the others made their way among the trees until they came to a clearing on the riverbank. Here, Rama and Lakshmana built a little hut of yellow bamboo, with a roof made with dried, golden leaves of the bo tree.

The three young people took up their life in the forest. They ate fruits and berries that grew on the trees and bushes. Their beds were piles of dried leaves. Their ears were filled with the calls of jungle birds, and the chatter of monkeys in the treetops. Their eyes were filled with the green and gold of sunlight shining upon leaves.

One morning, Sita stepped to the doorway of the hut. In the clearing between the hut and the forest stood a beautiful golden-skinned deer. It gazed upon Sita with shining eyes.

"Oh, Rama my husband! Lakshmana my brother! Catch this beautiful deer for me, please," whispered Sita. "I want it for a pet."

The deer trotted into the forest. Rama and Lakshmana ran after it. They were quickly out of sight.

Almost at once, an old, bent man came out of another part of the forest and hobbled toward Sita. In his hand was a begging bowl which he humbly held out to her. In pity, Sita took up a handful of berries from inside the hut and reached out to put them in the old beggar's bowl.

But suddenly, he seized her in a grip of iron! The old man's bent body vanished, and in his place stood a tall man with eyes that glowed like red-hot coals!

"I am Ravana, king of the Rakshas," hissed the man. Sita screamed in terror, for the Rakshas were evil demons who hated humans and delighted in causing grief and fear! Too late, Sita realized that the deer had been a trick to lure Rama and Lakshmana away, so that Ravana could capture her.

She was helpless in Ravana's grip. He carried her to the edge of the forest, where stood a golden chariot drawn by two winged horses. Holding Sita tightly, Ravana sprang into the chariot. Then, flapping their big wings, the horses carried the chariot into the sky.

As the chariot rose upward, a great eagle came gliding toward it. This was Jatayu, the eagle king. He had seen Ravana capture Sita, and now came to try to help her. But as he swooped at the chariot, Ravana thrust a

spear into his body. The wounded eagle plunged to the earth like a falling stone. The flying chariot sped onward until it vanished from sight in the blue sky.

Shortly, Rama and Lakshmana came hurrying back to the hut. They knew they had been tricked, for the golden deer had vanished before their eyes. They peered around the clearing and looked into the hut, anxiously calling Sita's name.

Suddenly, they heard a weak voice call out, "Rama!" Hurrying toward the sound, they found Jatayu, the eagle king, lying crumpled at the edge of the forest.

"Rama, your wife has been stolen by Ravana, king of the Rakshas," whispered the bird. "He has taken her toward the south, in his flying chariot." Those were the brave bird's last words. The spirit of life left his body.

Sadly, the two men buried him. Then, they set out at once through the forest, heading south. Rama was wild with grief over Sita's loss, but he was determined to find and rescue her.

For days the two men traveled through the green and gold forest. One morning they came to a broad clearing among the trees. In the clearing stood two monkeys dressed in rich clothing, decorated with jewels.

"Who are you?" called one of the monkeys. "Why are you traveling through the land of the monkey people?"

"I am Prince Lakshmana of Kosala," answered Lakshmana. "This is my brother, Prince Rama. His wife has been stolen by Ravana, king of the Rakshas, and we seek to find her. But, who are you?"

"This is Sugriva, king of the monkeys," said the monkey who had spoken. "And I am Hanuman, the general of his armies."

"I will help you find your wife, Prince Rama," said

King Sugriva. "For we monkeys, too, despise the evil Rakshas! My armies number in the tens of thousands. I shall send them throughout the land to find where the Princess Sita is being held prisoner."

King Sugriva divided his armies into four groups. Each group was sent in a different direction—one north, one south, one east, and one west. Through forests, over streams and rivers, across hills and valleys scurried the monkey warriors, seeking news of the beautiful Sita.

The leader of the group that headed south was Hanuman. Onward and onward he led his warriors, until at last they came to the edge of the sea.

"Now we must turn back," said one of the monkey warriors, sadly. "We can go no farther."

"But it may be that Princess Sita has been taken across this sea," said Hanuman, peering over the water. "There is a land far in the distance. I shall use my magic to go there."

Powerful, indeed, was the magic of Hanuman. Into the air he sprang, and with a single leap crossed the sea and came down in the far land. He saw at once that it was the fabled land of Lanka, home of the Rakshas!

Before him lay a great and beautiful city, through which moved crowds of the evil Rakshas. Hanuman waited until nightfall, then he stole into the city. Keeping in the shadows and moving quietly, he searched for some sign of Princess Sita.

In the center of the city rose a splendid palace. Hanuman knew this was the dwelling of King Ravana.

Into the great building the brave monkey crept. He searched everywhere, peering into every room. But he did not find the princess.

Hanuman left the palace and found himself in a lovely garden bathed with moonlight. A high wall surrounded the garden, and in a dark corner crouched a huddled figure. Hanuman crept nearer and saw that it was a woman. She was crying. His heart took an excited bound. Could this weeping woman be Sita?

Suddenly, a tall figure came striding into the garden. It was Ravana! He halted before the woman, and spoke.

"I will give you one last chance, Princess Sita," he said. "Give up your husband, Prince Rama, and become my wife—or else you will be slain!"

"Rama is my only love and I will not give him up even though you slay me," said Sita, proudly. "But he will come and save me!"

Ravana laughed scornfully. "Rama will never find you," he said. "He does not know where you are." He bent over her and scowled. "You have only two more weeks to make up your mind! Become my wife, or else you will become meat on the table of a Raksha feast!" He turned and strode away.

"Alas, what shall I do?" sobbed Sita. "What if Rama cannot find me in time? I don't want to be eaten by the Rakshas!"

"Do not give up hope, Princess," whispered Hanuman from his hiding place. "I will tell Rama where you are. He will come for you."

"Who are you?" asked Sita, peering into the darkness.

"I am Hanuman of the monkey people," he answered, stepping out so that she could see him. "I am Rama's friend. I shall go now and tell him I have found you. He will return with a great army of monkey warriors to conquer the Rakshas and free you!"

Then, using his magic again, Hanuman leaped across the sea and rejoined his warriors. They hurried back across the land, to where Rama and Lakshmana anxiously waited. The other armies had returned from the north, east, and west with no word of Sita, and Rama was wild with worry. But when Hanuman announced that he had found her in Lanka, across the sea, Rama was overjoyed. At once, the two men and the vast army of monkeys set out for the south.

When they reached the sea, most of the monkeys wondered how they would cross the water, for they had no boats. But Rama went to the edge of the sea and spoke.

"Spirit of the sea," he cried, "I ask your help. We must cross your water to reach the land of Lanka,

where my wife is held prisoner by the evil Rakshas. Will you help us?"

The surface of the water began to shimmer and sparkle, and a voice spoke. It was like the sound of waves hissing in toward shore.

"Rama," said the voice, "there is nothing I can do to help you cross my water. I am deep and vast, and cannot change what I am. But you have the means to cross me. Let each monkey gather rocks and logs and drop them into my water. They will pile up and form a great bridge."

By the tens of thousands, the monkeys spread out over the land. From a nearby forest they carried great logs and branches. From a nearby mountain they brought rocks and boulders. They poured these things into the water. Working day and night for five days, the monkeys built a long bridge that stretched across the sea to Lanka.

Across the bridge the monkey army marched with a sound like the rumble of thunder. From afar, the Rakshas heard them coming and grew afraid. When the monkeys reached the gate of the Raksha city, they set up a great shout of "Long live Rama!" The city walls shuddered, and the Rakshas trembled at the sound. But Sita laughed for joy to hear it.

In dreadful fury, the Rakshas rushed forth to do battle. Their commander was Indrajit, the son of Ravana, who was himself a magician of mighty power. His shining chariot was drawn by eight horses, and he guided them with reins that sparkled with diamonds.

Forward to meet their foes swept Rama, Lakshmana, and the brave monkey warriors of King Sugriva. Terrible beyond telling was the battle! The air was pierced by ten thousand spears and arrows from the men and the Rakshas. The courageous monkeys hurled stones and tree limbs. From sunrise until well into the night, the awful battle raged.

Where Rama and Lakshmana fought, the Raksha warriors died by the scores and hundreds. The men and the courageous and stout-hearted monkey warriors pushed their foes back. Then did Indrajit call upon his magic. He reached for his most terrible weapon, the Snake Arrow, and fitted it to his bow. Drawing back the bowstring, he loosed the arrow.

As the magic arrow sped through the air, it separated into eighty-four million pieces. Each piece became a poisonous snake with a darting tongue! Upon Rama and Lakshmana fell this host of dreadful serpents, winding around the two men and pinning them to the ground! The bodies of Rama and his brother were filled with the burning poison of the serpents!

From the monkeys there arose a great wail, and they drew back. They feared their leaders were dead, and they had lost heart to keep up the battle. Indrajit, believing he was victorious, gave a shout of joy. Turning his chariot, he drove back into the city. The Raksha warriors followed him, their cheers echoing through the night.

Great, indeed, was the wailing of the monkeys. The sound of it reached around the world. It was heard by Garuda, the giant king of the birds and mortal enemy of all snakes. With the speed of a lightning bolt, Garuda flew to Lanka. When his huge shadow fell upon the snakes that bound Rama and Lakshmana, the serpents, hissing with fear, crawled off to hide.

Thus the two heroes were freed. But they were still near death from the poison that burned in their bodies. However, an old monkey named Jambhava knew a cure for the poison—the scent of some flowers that grew on a mountaintop at the roof of the world. With one of his magical leaps, Hanuman sprang to the distant mountain and returned with a great pile of the blossoms. Their fragrance filled the nostrils of Rama and his brother. The poison left their bodies and the two men rose to their feet.

Now the monkeys gave a great cheer. Within the city, the Rakshas heard the cheers and realized that they

had not won victory after all. They knew then that their two greatest foes still lived. Once again, the Raksha warriors, led by Indrajit, came storming out of the city.

Long the battle raged. Then, suddenly, a terrible cry of grief and fear went up from the Raksha warriors. Their leader, the mighty magician Indrajit, had been slain by the courageous and splendid Lakshmana!

The Rakshas fled into the city and closed fast the gate against their foes. Great was the grief and rage of King Ravana when he learned of the death of his son Indrajit. Arming himself, he sprang into his chariot and led his warriors forth once more.

But now the warriors on each side held back. They saw that this battle must be between Rama and Ravana alone. Now must the evil Raksha King Ravana meet the good and noble Prince Rama in a fight to the death. The two mighty warriors hurled themselves at each other!

The very winds seemed to pause and wait, and the sun blazed down upon the plain like a great golden eye. The earth shook and trembled as the two mighty warriors strove against each other. Again and again, Rama was pierced by the spear of Ravana, and time after time, Rama's spear drew the blood of Ravana. At last, the two warriors drew apart, faint and weary.

Great was the concern of Rama. He saw that he could not slay Ravana no matter how fiercely he struck, for the evil Raksha was protected by magic. But Rama himself was too weak and wounded to do battle much longer. Somehow, he must slay Ravana quickly, or he himself would be slain. If that were to happen, the sorrowing Sita would remain a prisoner of the Rakshas forever!

But while the brave Rama and the grim Ravana had
battled, Hanuman had crept unseen into the Raksha
city. Quickly, the courageous monkey hero hurried to
the palace of Ravana. For there, he knew, was kept the
Dart of Death, the most powerful of magic weapons.
With it Rama could surely slay the wicked Ravana!

Seizing the magical object, Hanuman made his way
back out of the city. Speeding to the side of the weak
and weary Rama, he gave him the awful weapon.

Grimly did Rama fit the Dart of Death to his great
bow. Upon this weapon rested his fate, and the fate of
the beautiful Sita. Raising the bow, he stretched the
string to its utmost and sent the magical arrow speeding
through the sky. As the arrow flew, it sent forth flashes
of lightning and billows of smoke. Like a star that
flames through the night sky it sped. It pierced deep
into the iron heart of the evil King Ravana, striking him
dead!

Then from the monkey warriors of King Sugriva rose
a thundering shout of triumph. And from the Raksha
host arose a great cry of pain and grief. As one, the
Raksha warriors threw down their weapons in surrender
to the courageous and noble Prince Rama, their
conqueror.

Thus, with the help of his brother Lakshmana, the
monkey hero Hanuman, and the courageous monkey

warriors of King Sugriva, did Rama free his wife, the
beautiful Sita, from her captivity. In time, Rama, Sita,
and Lakshmana returned to the land of Kosala. Rama's
brother Bharata gladly gave up the throne so that
Rama might be king. Long and well did Rama rule, and
richly and nobly did he reward the monkey people for
their great help.

The Saving of Tam Lin

In many of the stories called fairy tales, the fairies are tiny, humanlike creatures. Sometimes they play pranks on people, but usually they are harmless. Sometimes they're even helpful.

But in many of the old, old tales and legends of Scotland, Ireland, Wales, and England, fairies are often as large as people. They are dangerous, magical creatures that do great harm. People were afraid of them!

The story of Tam Lin is an old Scottish ballad (song) about a brave girl who defied the dangerous power of the fairies in order to save the man she loved.

73

The Saving of Tam Lin

In a wee cottage near a wide forest in Scotland lived a farmer and his wife and daughter. The daughter's name was Janet. As soon as Janet was old enough to understand, her parents warned her not to go into the forest. It was well known that Fairy Folk roamed these woods—and there was no telling what they might do to someone they met.

As a child, Janet stayed far away from the woods. But as she grew older, she strayed nearer. And when she was finally a grown woman, she decided she wasn't a bit afraid of the Fairy Folk. So, one day she walked into the woods to pick wild roses.

She had hardly been in the forest any time at all when a young man, dressed all in green, stepped out from among the trees and smiled at her. He had a very nice smile, and she was soon talking with him as if he were an old friend. He told her his name was Tam Lin.

After that, Janet went into the woods each day to be with Tam Lin, for she found that she liked him very much. One day, while they were walking, Janet asked

Tam Lin to come home with her and meet her parents. Sadly, Tam shook his head.

"I cannot leave the forest, Janet," he told her. "There is a spell upon me. I am a mortal, like you, but I belong to the Fairy Folk. Long ago, when I was a little boy, they stole me from my home, carried me to Fairyland, and bound me with enchantments. By day, I can walk and hunt in these woods, but at night I must return to Fairyland."

Janet was saddened to hear that, for she was beginning to hope that perhaps she and Tam Lin could be married. But she kept coming into the woods each day, and she and Tam were happy just being together.

But one day in late autumn when Tam stepped out of the trees to meet her, Janet saw that he was far from happy. His eyes were sad and fearful, and his mouth was grim.

"Tam, what is the matter?" she anxiously asked him.

"Every seven years the Fairy Folk must make a sacrifice to the dark spirits," said he. "This is the year the sacrifice is to be made. The time for it is drawing near—and I have been chosen to be the sacrifice."

"No, Tam!" she shrieked. "You must flee! You must flee now, while there is still time!"

"You know I cannot," he reminded her, sadly. "I cannot break the spell that keeps me here."

"There must be some way of saving you," she wept.

"There is a way," he said, "if it can be done. On the night of the sacrifice the Fairy Queen will remove the spell so that I can leave the forest and travel with the Fairies to the Hill of the Circle of Stones. If someone who loves me can wait at the crossroads until I arrive, and can then seize me and hold me for the time of twenty-one heartbeats—I shall be free from the Fairies forever."

"I can do that!" Janet exclaimed.

"It will not be as easy as you think, Janet," he said, grimly. "The night of the sacrifice is Samhain Eve—the time when all the evil and terrifying creatures of darkness are free to roam. You will be out in the darkness alone, among them!"

Janet shivered. But then she lifted her head, proudly. "I will be afraid," she said. "But I will do it."

"There is even more," Tam Lin told her. "When you seize me, the Fairies will use their magic to make you let me go. It will be fearsome, painful, and dangerous. They will make you see and hear and feel dreadful, terrifying things. You will want to let go of me, and run and hide. You will want to let go of me to stop the terrible pain!"

"I will hold you fast no matter what they do," she promised, looking into his eyes. "I will set you free."

"I think that perhaps you can," said Tam, becoming more hopeful. "You are very brave! But I will hope and pray that you do not come to harm on Samhain Eve, trying to save me."

The days passed, and the day of Samhain Eve (which we call Halloween) arrived. As soon as the sun set, most people went into their homes. Fearing the creatures that roamed in the darkness that night, they stayed inside with the doors barred. But Janet slipped out of the house without her parents knowing it, and hurried to the crossroads. There she crouched, huddled in her cloak, trying to make herself as hard to see as possible.

She was in dreadful danger! All around her she could hear strange sounds. At times, in the moonlight, she glimpsed things that made her heart stand still in terror! But, fortunately, she was not discovered by any of the dreadful creatures that were moving through the night.

It was nearing midnight when she heard the sounds of many people coming up the road toward her. Soon, she could see who was making the sounds. It was a long procession of the Fairy Folk, taking Tam Lin to be sacrificed. The Fairies rode fine horses and were dressed like rich lords and ladies. Their faces were beautiful, but their eyes were like chips of silvery ice!

Then, Janet saw Tam Lin. He was dressed in a white robe, and he walked sadly, his head down, between two black-robed Fairy Wizards. Janet waited until he reached the place where she was crouched. Then, she leaped up, sprang forward, and threw her arms around him.

The Fairies halted. Their faces shone with anger and they hissed like serpents. The Wizards raised their arms, and in voices like rustling whispers they began to chant magical spells.

Suddenly, Tam Lin changed. He was no longer a man.
He had become a huge, shaggy, yellow-eyed wolf. He
snarled, and snapped at Janet with sharp fangs!

Startled and frightened, Janet almost let go of him.
Then she remembered that if she did let go, Tam would
remain a prisoner of the Fairies—and would be
sacrificed. She closed her eyes and held him even more
tightly.

Again, he changed. He became a slimy, wormlike

thing that wriggled and twisted in Janet's arms. She shuddered in horror, but she gritted her teeth and held on.

Then Tam Lin became a metal statue that glowed red-hot, as if it had just come out of a furnace. Janet shrieked as the hot metal seared her skin—but she kept her arms around the statue despite the pain.

Now the glowing statue became a huge lump of ice, hard as iron and as cold as cold could be. The terrible cold bit into Janet's body more fiercely than fire. Again she screamed in pain—but she did not loosen her arms.

The lump of ice became a huge bat. It beat Janet's head and shoulders with its hard, leathery wings, trying to fly away. Dazed and bruised, Janet held on.

Then Janet heard the Fairies wail and shriek. There was a bright flash of light, and they all vanished. She realized that Tam Lin had changed once more. He was now himself again. The time of twenty-one heartbeats had gone by, and she had held onto Tam without once letting go. He was saved. She had braved the dreadful dangers of Samhain Eve, and the terrible spells of the Fairy Wizards. She had won!

It was past midnight, Samhain Eve was over, and the night was safe. Janet and Tam Lin walked slowly through the moonlight to Janet's home. A few days later, they were married. And never again did Tam or Janet ever go near Carterhaugh Wood, the home of the Fairy Folk!

The Journey to Find the Sun

This story is an old, old legend of the Blackfoot
Indians of North America. The Blackfoot once lived
in an area that stretched from what is now the state
of Montana in the United States to central Alberta
in Canada. This is an area of great plains, where
buffalo once roamed.

The young man in this legend is like the heroes of
many Indian legends. He does not think much of
himself. He does not believe he will be able to do the
things he must try to do. However, he keeps trying,
and he is brave when he has to be. He is the kind of
hero that many Indians liked best.

The Journey to Find the Sun

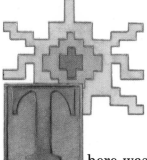here was once a very beautiful girl whose father was wealthy. His buffalo-skin bags were always filled with food, and there were piles of fine fur robes in his tepee. He had many dogs to carry his belongings when the tribe moved to a new camping place.

Many young men wanted to marry the girl, and many did ask her to marry them. But always the girl said that she did not want a husband. Her father began to worry about this.

"Why," he asked her one day, "do you not marry? Many of the finest young men have asked you. They are brave, they are handsome, but still you turned them all away."

"Father, I must tell you my secret," said the girl. "I have been told by the Sun, The-Person-Who-Is-Above, that I belong to him! He has told me that I will live a long life and be happy, but I must never marry."

"You must do as he says then, of course," said her father.

Now in the tribe at that time there was a young man

who was as poor as the beautiful girl was wealthy. His
parents and all his relatives were dead, and so he had
no one to give him any help. His clothes were worn and
shabby. He had no tepee of his own. But he was a kind
and good-natured person. He was also very nice looking,
except that he had a scar on one cheek. Because of this,
he was known as Scar-on-the-Face.

The other young men often made fun of Scar-on-the-
Face. He would usually just smile and pay little
attention to them. But one day, several of them began
to tease him about the beautiful girl.

"Why don't you ask her to marry *you*?" they said.
"She has refused us, who are handsome and wealthy.
Perhaps she would prefer you, who are poor and all
scarred up."

The fact is that the young man was deeply in love
with the girl. He would have given anything to have her
for his wife. But he had never dared to ask her. Now,
however, the words of the young men made him think

about it. "Why *don't* I ask her?" he said to himself. "I have nothing to lose. She can only refuse me. But— maybe she won't."

Scar-on-the-Face went down to the river, to where the women came to get water for their families, and waited. When the girl came, he stepped in front of her. She stopped, and looked up at him.

"I know that many men have asked you to marry them," he said to her. "They were handsome and they were rich, but you refused all of them. I do not think I am handsome, and I am far from rich. I have no tepee, no fine clothes, no fur robes, no dogs. I do not even have a family. But I ask you to marry me."

The girl put her head down and without looking at him said words that filled him with joy. "I will gladly be your wife, Scar-on-the-Face. It does not matter that you are poor. My mother and grandmothers will make us a tepee. My father will give you dogs and fur robes. My family will be your family.

"But there is something you must do first," she went on. "I belong to the Sun, and he has told me I must never marry. I did not care when those other men were asking me. But now I care. You must go to the Sun and tell him that I wish to be free to marry you. If he agrees, tell him to take the scar from your face. If you return without it, I will know that I am free and that we can be married."

The young man hung his head. "Your first words gave me so much joy I thought my heart would fly into the sky," he said. "But now, my heart is like a heavy stone. How can I go to the Sun? Who knows where his tepee is? Who knows the trail that leads to him?"

The girl touched his hand. "You must find him," she said softly. "There is no other way for us." Then she left him and went down to the river.

Scar-on-the-Face stood for a long time, thinking. How could he possibly find his way to the Sun? It was impossible. It was not even worth trying.

"But that is what I thought about the girl," he said to himself. "I thought it was not worth trying to ask her to marry me. But it was worth it, after all. Perhaps this will be worth doing, too! If I fail, I have nothing to lose, for she could not marry me anyway. But if I at least try, I may be able to find the Sun. Then everything I want will be mine."

The next morning, Scar-on-the-Face filled a

buffalo-skin bag with dried meat and set out on his journey. For many days, he traveled across the prairie. He came to a small river and swam across it. On the other side, he found himself in a forest and walked through it. His food soon ran out, but he lived on roots, berries, nuts, and small birds and animals he killed.

Each night he made camp and slept. One night, he camped beside the den of a gray wolf. "Ho, Brother," said the wolf, coming out of the den to greet him. "You are far from your hunting grounds. Where are you going?"

"I am searching for the Sun," said Scar-on-the-Face. "Do you know where his tepee stands?"

"I roam far when I hunt each night by the light of the moon," said the wolf. "I know of distant hills and valleys, forests and plains. But I have never seen the Sun's tepee in any of those places. A day's journey from here there dwells a bear who is a greater traveler than I am. Go and ask him if he has ever seen the Sun's home. Perhaps he has."

Scar-on-the-Face traveled all the next day. As darkness was falling, he came to the bear's den. The bear came out to see him.

"You are a long way from the land of your people," said the bear. "Why have you traveled so far?"

"I must find the Sun and speak with him," Scar-on-the-Face told him. "Can you show me which trail to take?"

"That is a thing I do not know," said the bear. "Far do I roam, but never have I seen the tepee of the Sun.

But in a woods a day's journey from here there dwells a wolverine who has traveled far. He may be able to help you."

The next day, Scar-on-the-Face traveled on. At nightfall he came to the woods. It was too dark to look for the wolverine's lair, so he stood and called out, "Wolverine, my Brother, I need your help."

Shortly, the wolverine came shuffling out from among the trees. "I am here, my Brother," the wolverine said. "How can I help you?"

"Many days have I journeyed in search of the Sun," said Scar-on-the-Face. "The girl I want to marry belongs to him, and I must tell him she wishes to be free to become my wife. But I cannot find the way to him."

"I know the way," said the wolverine. "Tomorrow I will show you the trail."

Scar-on-the-Face went to sleep happy that night. The next morning, the wolverine led him through the woods until they came to a trail winding among the trees.

"Follow this trail to the Great Water," said the wolverine. "It is upon the other side of the Great Water that the Sun makes his home."

Scar-on-the-Face followed the trail all that day and camped upon it at night. The next day he set out again. The trail left the forest behind and crossed a vast plain. And, finally, it reached the Great Water.

Scar-on-the-Face stared in wonder. Never had he seen so much water. It seemed to go on and on forever. He could not even see across it to the other side.

"I cannot swim across this," said Scar-on-the-Face. "And there are no trees nearby with which to make a raft. There is no way for me to get across."

He sat down on the bank and hung his head in despair. "I have no food," he said. "My moccasins are worn out. I cannot cross the Great Water. I cannot return to my home. I will stay here and die!"

Just then, two large swans came swimming across the Great Water toward him. "Why are you here, Brother?" asked one. "You are a long, long way from the land of your people."

"I have been searching for the Sun," said Scar-on-the-Face. "But here my trail ends. I cannot cross the Great Water."

"Ho, we can take you across easily," said the swan. "Come into the water and take hold of us."

Scar-on-the-Face waded into the Great Water, between the two swans. He put an arm around each of them. Then they began to swim across the Great Water, easily carrying him along with them.

A long time later they reached the other side of the Great Water. "Here is where you will find the one you seek, The-Person-Who-Is-Above," said one of the swans. "Follow the trail."

Scar-on-the-Face thanked them and started up the

trail. His heart was singing, for he felt he would soon find the one he had been seeking so long.

Suddenly, he caught sight of some things lying beside the trail. There was a fine bow made of smooth, silvery wood and decorated with tufts of colored fur. There was a quiver of antelope skin, full of fine arrows. There was a buffalo-hide shield, painted in bright colors and decorated with feathers and colored porcupine quills. Scar-on-the-Face had never seen such beautiful weapons. He looked at them for a time, but he did not touch any of them. Then he went on along the trail. After a time he saw someone coming toward him. It was a young, handsome man in bright clothing.

"Ho, stranger," said the young man. "Did you see a pile of weapons as you came along the trail?"

"Yes," replied Scar-on-the-Face. "But I did not touch them. If they are yours, you will find them as you left them."

"You are an honest person," said the man. "Who are you? Why are you here?"

"I am called Scar-on-the-Face. I am seeking the Sun."

"My name is Star-of-the-Early-Morning," said the young man. "The Sun is my father. Come with me and you shall meet him."

Overjoyed, Scar-on-the-Face went with him. They came to a great tepee, which was the largest and most beautifully painted tepee Scar-on-the-Face had ever seen. Inside it were many marvelous things, such as shining fur robes, fine weapons, and buffalo-skin bags bulging with food. Among all these things sat a beautiful woman.

"This is my mother, the Moon," said Star-of-the-Early-Morning.

"You are welcome here," said the Moon. "But why have you made such a long, hard journey from the land of your people?"

"I have come to see your husband, the Sun," Scar-on-the-Face told her. "There is something I must ask of him."

"You will soon meet him," said the Moon. "For I see him coming, even now."

Bright light shone in the tepee as the Sun came into it. He stopped and looked at Scar-on-the-Face. "Who is this person?" he asked.

"I met him on the trail this morning," said Star-of-the-Early-Morning. "I know he is a good person. I left my weapons where he could have stolen them, but he did not even touch them."

"Stay with us for a while," said the Sun to Scar-on-the-Face. "It will be good for my son to have another young person here who can be his friend."

So Scar-on-the-Face stayed in the tepee of the Sun that night. He decided not to ask the Sun about the girl for a while. He was a little afraid to.

In the morning, the Sun left to go and bring light to the earth. "Let us go and hunt, my friend," said Star-of-the-Early-Morning.

But before they left, the Moon spoke to Scar-on-the-Face. "I ask that you watch over my son," she said. "Keep him from going too near the Great Water. I have had many sons, but he is the last. The others were all killed by the terrible Birds of Evil that live beside the Great Water. They will kill Star-of-the-Early-Morning, too, if they can."

Scar-on-the-Face promised to guard Star-of-the-Early-Morning well. The two young men left the tepee. All morning they hunted in the forest, but they did not see one animal.

At last they found the tracks of a deer. "Let us follow these tracks," cried Star-of-the-Early-Morning.

But Scar-on-the-Face saw that the tracks led toward the Great Water. "We must not follow them," he said. "They will take you into danger."

However, Star-of-the-Early-Morning would not listen to his friend. He began to follow the trail of the deer. Badly worried, Scar-on-the-Face went with him.

Suddenly, they found themselves out of the forest.

There before them lay the Great Water. And coming swiftly toward them were the Birds of Evil! They were huge and black, with fierce red eyes and sharp, blood-red beaks and claws. They made horrible squawks and screeching noises as they came.

Quickly, Scar-on-the-Face stepped in front of Star-of-the-Early-Morning and raised his spear. In an instant, the birds were all about him. Their wings beat at him, their bills tore at him, their claws ripped at him. He put one hand up in front of his face to protect his eyes and began to slash and jab with his spear.

Long did Scar-on-the-Face battle the Birds of Evil to save his friend. After a time he was weak and bleeding from many wounds—but all the evil birds lay dead upon the ground.

"You have saved me, Scar-on-the-Face," said Star-of-the-Early-Morning. "Let us cut off the heads of these birds and take them to show to my mother and father. Then they will know that I am now safe forever."

When the Moon saw the heads of all the dead Birds of Evil she cried for joy. When the Sun came home that night, she told him what had happened. She begged him to reward Scar-on-the-Face for saving their son.

"Indeed, you have given the Moon and me great happiness," said the Sun to Scar-on-the-Face. "You deserve a great reward. What can I give you?"

"I ask two things," said Scar-on-the-Face. "First,

there is a girl of my tribe who would marry me, but you have told her that she belongs to you and may not marry. I beg you to set her free so she can be my wife."

"I know that girl," said the Sun. "She is good and she is wise, which is why I made her mine. Such women are dear to me and I give them long life. But now I give her to you, and you both shall live a long time. Now, what is the second thing you wish to ask for?"

"I beg you to take this scar off my face as a sign to the girl that she may marry me," said Scar-on-the-Face.

"That is easy to do," said the Sun. He rubbed his hand over the young man's face and the scar vanished. "Now I will show you a short way home," said the Sun. "It is the sky trail—the trail of stars."

But before they let him leave, Star-of-the-Early-Morning and the Moon gave Scar-on-the-Face presents of beautiful clothes and fine weapons. And again, the Sun and his family thanked the young man for saving the life of Star-of-the-Early-Morning and making him safe forever.

Then Scar-on-the-Face set out on the sky trail. He traveled swiftly through the darkness among the glittering stars. By morning he was standing on a small hill that overlooked the camp of his people.

Scar-on-the-Face walked into the village. He was dressed in beautiful clothing of fine animal skins, decorated with colored feathers and porcupine quills. He carried a fine bow made of shining wood, and a brightly painted shield. No one recognized him. Everyone wondered who this handsome, wealthy stranger was.

He went to the tepee in which the girl lived, and waited. After a time, she came out and her eyes fell upon him. She recognized him at once. "You found the way to the Sun," she said, her eyes shining with happiness.

"The way was long and hard," he said. "I thought I would die before I found it. But I was helped by friendly animals, and I finally reached the Sun's tepee. He has set you free so that we can be married." He turned his head to show the girl that the scar was gone from his cheek.

So the young man and the girl were married. And, as the Sun had promised, they had a long and happy life together.

The Creature in the Forest

In the south of France, on the Rhône River, there is a town named Tarascon. For hundreds of years, on June 28 each year, an odd parade has taken place in Tarascon. A huge figure of a dragon, made of paper or cloth, is carried through the town. In front of it walks a young woman.

The figure of the dragon represents a dragon called the Tarasque, for which the town is named. The young woman represents Saint Martha, a Christian saint. According to a legend that's probably more than sixteen hundred years old, the Tarasque once lived near Tarascon and often preyed upon the people of the town. It was finally conquered by Saint Martha. The following story is based on that old, old legend of Saint Martha and the Tarasque.

105

The Creature in the Forest

It was night. Starlight sparkled faintly on the broad, dark surface of the Mediterranean Sea. In the distance lay a long black streak that spread across the horizon—the southern coast of France.

Something was swimming in the sea, leaving a silvery wake in the water. It was only a black shape in the darkness, but it seemed to be very large and long, with two big, green, glowing eyes. It swam steadily toward the coast of France until it came to the broad mouth of the Rhône River. It swam up the river, moving inland, where towns and cities stood. After a time, it came to a part of the river that ran through a forest. Leaving the water, the creature clambered up the riverbank into the darkness among the trees.

Next morning, the sun rose on the forest and on the little town of Nerluc, which stood at the forest's edge. A woodcutter, his ax over his shoulder, walked slowly out of the town and into the woods. He intended to cut down and chop up a sturdy oak. He hoped to sell the wood to carpenters, who could make it into furniture.

But that evening the woodcutter did not come home with his load of wood. The next morning, his worried wife asked two of his friends to go into the woods and search for him. They went—and never returned.

The people of Nerluc began to get worried. It was clear that there was something dangerous in the forest! Was it wolves? Bears? Bandits?

A narrow road wound through the forest. One day, a group of people from another town trudged along this road on their way to Nerluc. They came to a very dark, gloomy part of the woods, near the river. The tree branches, thick with leaves, shut out the sunlight. A high, rocky cliff rose on one side of the road.

Suddenly, without warning, a huge, horrible shape shot out of the gloom and leaped upon the little group of travelers! They saw glowing eyes, a huge mouth filled with teeth as large as bulls' horns, and a great, scaly body—a dragon!

The people shrieked and tried to flee, but the dragon was as quick as a cat chasing a mouse. Only one man managed to get away. Screaming with fear, he ran through the forest until he began to gasp for breath. A short time later he came staggering into Nerluc, his clothing torn and his eyes wild.

"A dragon in the forest," he panted. "It attacked us. All the others were killed! Only I escaped."

The citizens of Nerluc stared at one another in dismay—a dragon in their forest!

The town council held a meeting. It ordered people to stop going into the forest to hunt or get wood. Word was sent to other towns, warning people not to travel through the forest. It was hoped that if the dragon couldn't find anyone to eat in the woods, it would soon go away.

A week passed. Then, in the middle of a silent, moonless night, the dragon came stalking into Nerluc! It had grown hungry waiting for food to come to it, and had finally decided to go to where it sensed there was plenty of food. The huge creature smashed down the wall of a house and devoured everyone inside! When it was finished, it lumbered back into the dark forest.

First thing in the morning, the town council held another meeting. "This monster will return again and again," warned the mayor. "So long as it lives, Nerluc, and all of us who live here, are in dreadful danger. The creature must be destroyed!"

Notices were tacked up throughout the town, asking
for brave, strong young men to volunteer to kill the
dragon. Sixteen men agreed to try. Armed with axes,
swords, and spears, they marched out into the forest to
seek the creature.

They found the dragon sleeping in a grove of ash
trees. Bravely, they attacked, stabbing with swords and
spears, and hacking with axes. But they quickly
discovered that their weapons would not even dent the
dragon's tough scales. The beast awoke, and in rage
began to fight back. Eight of the men were killed. The
others fled back to the town.

The councilors were now desperate. Holding another

meeting, they tried to think of some way of protecting
the town against the monster.

"We must get rid of it somehow," muttered the
mayor, gnawing his lip. "Otherwise everyone in Nerluc
will be eaten!" He shuddered.

"But what are we to do?" moaned one of the
councilors. "If the creature cannot be killed with
ordinary weapons, how can it be killed?"

"With magic?" suggested another councilor.

"There are no magicians in Nerluc," the mayor
pointed out. "And I do not know of any magicians in
any nearby towns."

"Hold!" exclaimed one of the councilors. "I have
heard that a great holy woman lives not far from here,
in the town of Sainte Marie de la Mer. Her name is
Martha, and it is said that she can perform miracles.
Perhaps she could overcome this beast with her
holiness."

"We must send someone to beg her to help us,"
declared the mayor.

Two of the councilors were picked to go to the holy
woman. They took a small boat down the river to
Sainte Marie de la Mer. Reaching the town, they asked
where the holy woman lived, and went at once to see
her.

Martha was a middle-aged woman with a pleasant
face. She listened with sympathy as they told her of
their town's dreadful problem.

"I know of this dragon," she said. "It often caused
trouble in the Holy Land, where I once lived. It is called
the Tarasque, and it is a most wicked creature indeed. I
will go back to Nerluc with you and do what I can to
help you get rid of the Tarasque."

Overjoyed, the two men took her to the boat and sailed back to Nerluc. The mayor, the other councilors, and a crowd of people were waiting on shore. Everyone bowed as Martha stepped off the boat.

"Our deepest thanks for coming to help us," said the mayor. He looked at her hopefully. "Do you have a plan for conquering the monster?"

"No," Martha told him. "I shall just go into the forest and look for the beast. When I find it, I'll do what I think is best."

The mayor pulled thoughtfully at his beard. "How many men will you want to take with you?"

"None," said Martha. "I don't want to risk having anyone else get hurt."

"I see," said the mayor. "Well, will you need any special weapon then?"

"I'll just take these," said Martha, showing him a bottle of holy water and a prayer book.

"Very well," said the mayor. "I certainly hope everything works out for you! When will you go to find the creature?"

"Right now," said Martha. "If I wait any longer, the Tarasque may have a chance to eat some other unlucky person."

Most of the townspeople followed her to the edge of the forest. They watched respectfully as she walked in among the trees. They were all amazed at her courage in going after the Tarasque all by herself, with nothing but holy water and a prayer book. However, many of them—and the mayor was one—feared she would be killed and eaten!

Martha, too, knew she was in deadly danger. She peered toward all sides as she walked through the trees,

hoping to see the Tarasque before it saw her. She felt
sure she could conquer it if she could catch it unawares.
But if it should leap upon her from behind, she would
have no more chance than any of the people who had
been eaten!

The part of the forest near the town was sunny and
pleasant. From time to time she heard a bird sing, and
that seemed a good sign to her. She didn't think birds
would stay close to such a wicked thing as the
Tarasque.

But as she walked farther into the forest, it grew
gloomier and more quiet. Martha tried to walk more
softly, so that her footsteps wouldn't make so much
noise. She peered about very carefully. She felt sure she
was getting close to the Tarasque. And, after a time, she
saw something white gleaming in the underbrush. She
looked closely. Bones—human bones—with the marks of
big, sharp teeth on them!

Martha now began to walk very carefully, on tiptoe.
Then, through the trees she saw something in the
distance. It looked like a huge, scaly body! Cautiously
she stole toward it. It was indeed the Tarasque,
standing in a clearing with its back to her.

Closer and closer to it she moved. When she was
nearly close enough to reach out and touch the
Tarasque's scaly body, she pulled the cork out of the
bottle of holy water.

Suddenly, the Tarasque's head shot up and turned to
look straight at Martha. The big green eyes glared at
her. The huge mouth, full of teeth like bulls' horns,
opened wide! With a quick prayer, Martha flung the
contents of the bottle onto the Tarasque's body.

For a moment, nothing happened. The Tarasque

seemed to freeze, motionless. Then it closed its mouth
and lowered its head, as if it were bowing to Martha!

She let out a sigh of relief. The Tarasque had been
made tame and helpless by the holy water. "Follow
me," she ordered it. Turning, she walked back through
the woods to Nerluc. The huge Tarasque lumbered
along behind her.

The people of Nerluc were amazed to see Martha
come out of the woods with the dragon. She led it into
the town square and told it to lie down. Then she
turned to the mayor.

"The Tarasque is now helpless and can do no harm," she said. "But it must be killed, in punishment for its wickedness. It can't be killed by swords or spears, but a strong man can kill it by hitting it on the head with a club."

So the Tarasque was put to death. Nerluc was saved by the goodness, holiness—and courage—of Martha. In later years, the people of Nerluc changed their town's name to Tarascon so that no one would ever forget the story of the Tarasque and Martha's bravery.

The Island
of the Ogres

This tale—the story of Momotaro, the Peach Boy, and his visit to the Island of Ogres—is one of the favorite stories of the children of Japan. It was first written down more than a thousand years ago, but is probably even much older than that.

Like many legends, the story of Momotaro may be based upon something that really happened. A long time ago there was a young Japanese prince. He commanded an army that was sent to conquer an island that was a stronghold of some troublesome bandits. Storytellers may have changed the prince into Momotaro, the Peach Boy, and turned the island of bandits into The Island of the Ogres.

117

The Island of the Ogres

ong, long ago, in the little village of Kurusu,
near the Kiso River, there lived an old woodcutter and
his old wife. They were poor, hard-working people, but
they were happy. They were glad to have a roof over
their heads and a bowl of rice for supper each
night—sometimes, even with a pickle.

But there was one thing that made them feel sad
from time to time. They had never had a child. More
than anything, they had wanted a little boy. But now,
they were too old.

One day, the old man went out into the forest to cut
wood. The old woman went down to the river to wash
clothes. She soaked each garment in the water, then she
rubbed and beat it against a flat stone to get it clean. It
was hard work, but she didn't mind. As she worked, she
hummed a tune and smiled at the beauty of the
sparkling water, the bright, green grass, and the graceful
willow trees bending over the river.

All at once she saw something floating down the river
toward her. As it came closer, she saw it was the biggest

peach she had ever seen—truly, an enormous peach! By reaching out over the water, she was able to pull the peach toward her and lift it out of the river.

She looked it over with delight. It was as soft as an emperor's silk robe, and as golden as the sunlight. It smelled delicious. She was sure it would taste sweeter than honey.

"I've never seen a peach as fine as this in all my years," said she to herself. "Just wait till my dear old husband sees it." She placed it carefully on the grass and went on with her work.

As the sun was setting, she took the clothing and the peach and started for home. At the door of the house she met her husband bringing home a huge load of wood on his back.

"I have a surprise for you, honorable husband," she told him with a smile.

"That's good news, honorable wife," he said, smiling back. "I worked hard today. A surprise will make my aching bones feel better. What is it?"

"This," said the old woman, showing him the peach.

His eyes grew wide. "Never have I seen such a splendid peach," he cried. "Where did you buy it?"

"That's the best part," said she. "I *found* it! It was floating down the stream."

"Remarkable," said the man. "Well, it will taste all the better because we didn't have to spend money for it! Let us share it."

Taking out his knife, he was about to slice the peach in half when it fell apart. The two old people saw an amazing sight. In the middle of the peach, instead of the seed there sat a beautiful little baby boy! He smiled and held out his arms to the man and woman.

"A baby boy! A son!" cried the old woman, picking up the baby and hugging him. "He has been given to us by the gods!"

They named the baby Momotaro—Little Peach Boy. They lovingly brought him up as their own son, and were never sad again.

The years passed, and Momotaro grew tall and strong. At the age of fifteen, he went to his parents.

"Mother and father," he said, "all these years you have taken care of me and given me your love. Now it is time for me to begin taking care of you. I must go away for a while, but when I come back I will bring such wealth that you will never have to worry about anything again!"

"But where are you going?" asked his mother.

"Far in the north is an island," said Momotaro.
"Upon the island lives a tribe of ogres. They are very
rich, but they often attack villages and rob and kill
people. I am going to conquer them and punish them,
and I will bring some of their riches back here for you."

The old man gasped in dismay. "I know of those
ogres, Momotaro. They have red skins and horns on
their heads—and they eat human flesh! How can you
possibly conquer them? You are but a boy!"

Momotaro smiled. "Ah, but remember that I am not
an ordinary boy, honorable father. I am the Peach Boy,
and I can do things no other boy can do!"

His father and mother knew this was true, and so they agreed to let him go. His mother made some rice balls for him to take so that he would have something to eat when he became hungry.

So, Momotaro set out. He was about one-fourth of the way to the Island of the Ogres when a large, rather thin-looking dog came running toward him.

"Do you have anything to eat?" whined the dog. "I am starving!"

"Of course," said Momotaro, and gave the dog a rice ball. After that the dog happily followed him.

Momotaro was about halfway to the Island of the Ogres when a rather thin monkey came skittering down a tree and ran up to him.

"Do you have anything to eat?" chattered the monkey. "I am starving!"

"Here," said Momotaro, and gave the monkey a rice ball. After that the monkey also followed him.

Momotaro was about three-fourths of the way to the Island of the Ogres when a large bird flew up out of a bush and landed on his shoulder.

"Do you have anything to eat?" chirped the bird. "I am starving!"

"Have a rice ball," said Momotaro, and gave her one. After that the bird stayed with him, riding on his shoulder.

Finally, Momotaro and his companions came to the seacoast. "What is *that*?" asked the dog, staring at all the water. "I have never seen such a big mud puddle!"

"That is the sea," Momotaro told him. "Now, we must find a way to get across it to the Island of the Ogres."

He looked around. There were no trees in sight with

which to build a raft. But there were many pieces of
driftwood lying on the beach. Momotaro had the
animals gather up all the driftwood they could find. He
made rope out of hair from the dog and monkey, and
used it to fasten the wood together to make a raft. Then
he and the animals climbed aboard and drifted out to
sea.

The sea was covered with a thick, white fog. It came
drifting all around the raft until Momotaro and the
animals felt as if they were inside a cloud. They
couldn't see any farther than the ends of their
noses—or, in the case of the bird, any farther than the
end of her beak.

But suddenly Momotaro thought he saw a dim gray
shape just ahead. Sure enough, rising out of the mist
was a gray, rocky island, and towering over the island
was a great gray castle. It was the Island of the Ogres!

Guiding the raft toward the shore, Momotaro and the
animals stepped onto the beach. With Momotaro in the
lead, they marched toward the castle. The castle was

surrounded by a high wall, and in the center of the wall was a tall gate. Momotaro pushed on the gate, but it was locked from inside.

"Fly up over the wall and see if there are any ogres around," he told the bird. She flew off. In a short time she was back.

"The ogres are all inside the castle," she said.

"Climb over the wall and unlock the gate," Momotaro said to the monkey. The monkey scampered up over the wall. After a moment Momotaro heard the sound of the big bar being pulled out of the way. When he pushed the gate, it opened easily. He and the dog marched inside.

Momotaro put his hands on his hips and lifted his head. "Ogres," he yelled, "Momotaro is here. I have come to put an end to your wickedness. Come out here and be conquered!"

With that, the ogres came rushing out of the castle. They were horrible-looking creatures! Their skins were bright red, and they had huge mouths, flat noses, and horns. Most of them carried big clubs that bristled with sharp spikes.

"Foolish boy!" roared Akandoji, the leader of the ogres. "Now we shall eat you and your silly animals!"

But Momotaro had explained to the animals what they had to do. "Attack!" he shouted. The bird flew at the ogres' faces, pecking at their eyes with her sharp bill. The dog dashed in and out among their feet, snapping and biting at their toes. And as if it were swinging through the trees, the monkey swung from one ogre to another, biting, scratching, punching, and choking them!

All this was simply too much for the ogres. "Ouch!

Stop it! Don't!" they howled, hopping up and down to
protect their feet and covering their faces with their
arms to protect their eyes. Momotaro ran forward and
seized Akandoji. The ogre chief struggled to get free,
but the Peach Boy was too strong for him.

"Do you give up?" cried Momotaro.

"Yes! Yes! Make them stop!" cried Akandoji.

"Only if you all pull out your horns," demanded
Momotaro. He knew that once an ogre lost its horns it
became tame and helpless.

So the ogres all began pulling out their horns. Soon
they were all standing quietly, guarded by the dog, the
monkey, and the bird. Momotaro saw that they were
now quite tame and would never again attack any of the
nearby villages—and never again eat any people!

But they still had to be punished for all the wicked

things they had done until now. "Bring out your treasure," ordered Momotaro. The ogres hurried into their castle and soon returned, each of them with an armful of wealth—gold, silver, coral, jewels, and rolls of costly cloth. They piled up all these things before Momotaro.

He picked out the best of all these treasures and loaded them into a cart. Then, with the bird and the dog pulling the cart, and Momotaro and the monkey pushing it, the conquerors set out for home.

And so Momotaro, the Peach Boy, brought riches back to his old father and mother as he had promised. They never had to worry again, for the rest of their lives. As for Momotaro, he became a rich, famous, and honored man.

Finn and
the Goblin

Tales about Finn MacCool have been told in Ireland
for more than a thousand years. The storytellers
gave the people the kind of hero they admired—a
strong, brave warrior who is also a poet, musician,
and man of wisdom. The stories take place about
seventeen hundred years ago, when people called
Celts, who spoke Gaelic, lived in Ireland. In Gaelic,
Finn's name is Fionn mac Cumhaill. *Fionn* means
"fair" and *mac* means "son of." In English, he is
called Finn MacCool.

The Celts called their land *Eriu*, after their sun
goddess. There were many small kingdoms, each
with its own ruler. There was also one ruler who was
the High King. The people all belonged to groups
called clans. Sometimes, two clans fought, as in this
tale of the boyhood of Finn.

Finn and the Goblin

umhaill mac Bascna was chief of Clan
Bascna. A tall, sturdy, blond-haired man, he was a
mighty warrior. He was captain of the Fianna, the army
of the High King. The Fianna was made up of the very
best warriors in all Eriu. Of course, the people of Clan
Bascna were enormously proud that their chief should
have such a high honor.

However, there were others who hated Cumhaill.
They were the people of Clan Morna, who thought one
of their leaders should be captain of the Fianna. With
tricks, lies, treachery, and cunning they tried to get rid
of Cumhaill. Great grew the hatred between the clans.

Finally, the hatred was so great that it exploded into
war. On a fresh spring morning, the men of the two
clans met in battle. The air shivered with the hiss of
hurled spears, the click and clash and clatter of swords,
and the screams of wounded and dying men.

In the end, Clan Bascna was defeated. Many of the
clan's greatest warriors lay dead upon the ground—and
one of them was Cumhaill himself. The warriors who

had not been killed fled and went into hiding to save their lives. Only the women of Clan Bascna were left, grieving for dead husbands, fathers, brothers, or sons.

Word of Cumhaill's death was brought to his wife, Murna. At once, she wrapped herself in her cloak and fled into the vast, shadowy green forest of Slieve Bloom. She knew the sons of Morna would soon seek for her with their spears, to end her life. They would want to wipe out Cumhaill's whole family, so that no one might try to take vengeance for his death.

With tears of grief flowing from her eyes, Murna wandered for a time through the wildwood. There, in the depths of the forest, she gave birth to a baby

boy—Cumhaill's son. She named him Demna. She knew that if Clan Morna warriors were to find her now, they would slay both her and the baby. He was not safe as long as he was with her.

Hidden away in the woods was a little cottage in which dwelt two wise women named Bovmall and Lia Luachra. Bovmall was the sister of dead Cumhaill, and thus was the baby's aunt. So Morna went to Bovmall and Lia.

"If the sons of Morna learn that this boy is Cumhaill's son, they will kill him," she told the two. "I beg of you, hide him here. Let no one know who he is."

"Fear not, sister-in-law," said Bovmall. "The child and his secret are safe with us."

So Demna grew up in the woods, reared by Bovmall and Lia. The forest creatures were his only playmates, and he learned from them. The squirrels taught him how to scamper up a tree as fast as an eye might blink. The rabbits in the glades showed him how to leap and dodge in a way that might save his life. From the fish in the forest ponds he learned how to swim. And from the deer of the woods he learned to run so swiftly that the very wind was left behind.

As he grew older, Demna learned other things. Bovmall and Lia sent him to stay for a time with a man named Fiacuil mac Cona. Fiacuil had been his father's comrade in arms and one of the greatest warriors of Clan Bascna. He had been hiding in the forest since the day of the dreadful battle. Now, he taught Demna how to cast a spear that never missed its target, and how to swing a sword so as to cut through the stoutest shield. Demna grew skilled in the use of a warrior's weapons.

The boy wandered far and wide through the forest.

Sometimes, he reached the very edge, where tiny villages lay. He would often steal into a village to play with children, and that was how he got a new name. Because of his light blond hair and pale skin, the children called him Fionn, which means "fair," or "blond."

All the while that Fionn, or Finn, was growing up he was in great danger. The men of Clan Morna had learned he was alive and were searching for him. They did not know where he was, but they would slay him if they found him.

Finally, the day came when Finn was full grown. Now he felt that he could do the thing he had wanted to do all his life—become captain of the Fianna, as was his father before him. He would set out for Tara, where the High King dwelt. Somehow he would get the High King to name him captain of the Fianna!

But first there was something he knew he needed. He was the swiftest of runners, the highest of leapers, and the best of swimmers. He was as strong as two men, feared nothing, and was skilled with every kind of weapon. But he knew that he also needed wisdom. So, he said his farewells to Bovmall and Lia and set out for the River Boyne, where there dwelt a famous wise man and poet by the name of Finegas.

Finn found Finegas living in a little hut on the riverbank. The young man bowed. "Master," said he, "I will keep your house cleaned and swept, chop your firewood, cook your meals, and do all else needed, if I may stay here and learn from you."

The old man smiled. "Stay," he invited. "What is your name?"

Finn felt it was better not to let the old man know he was Finn MacCool. He thought the men of Clan Morna might somehow learn that he was here and come to kill him. He wasn't afraid of them, but he feared that old Finegas might be hurt if there was a battle. "My name is Demna," he said.

From that time on, Finegas taught young Finn many things. He introduced him to the magic of poetry and the charm of music. He showed him the making of riddles and the solving of them. Each day, Finn's mind grew in knowledge and understanding.

"Why do you stay beside this river, Master, when

there are so many finer rivers in this land?" he asked
one day.

"In this river swims the fish that is known as the
Salmon of All Knowledge," Finegas told him.
"Whosoever eats that fish will gain all the knowledge of
the world! I stay here because it has been foretold that
some day I shall catch the Salmon of All Knowledge."

"I hope and pray you will catch it while I am with
you!" exclaimed Finn.

"Perhaps I shall," said Finegas, "perhaps I shall."

Days, weeks, and months rolled by. Then, one day,
Finegas went fishing as he often did. Suddenly, Finn
heard him call out. The young man ran to see what had

happened. He found Finegas sitting with a basket in his lap. In the basket lay a large orange and gold fish.

"I have caught it," said Finegas in a low, solemn voice. "I have caught the Salmon of All Knowledge!"

Finn let out a shout and leaped for joy. He was delighted that his old teacher would now be able to gain all the knowledge of the world. "I shall cook it for you," he said.

As Finn cooked the Salmon of All Knowledge, he thought of how wonderful was this moment for his beloved teacher. When the fish was done, he placed it before Finegas.

"Have you eaten of it?" asked Finegas.

"No," replied Finn. "It is yours to eat. I did but have a small taste. A blister formed while the fish was cooking and I pushed it down with my thumb. It gave me a burn, so I popped my thumb in my mouth to make it feel better. My, but it did taste good! You will know how good when you eat it."

Finegas looked at Finn and smiled. "There are two things that I know to be true," said Finegas. "One is that I shall never eat the Salmon of All Knowledge. And the other is that your name is not Demna. Your name is Finn MacCool."

"How can you know that?" cried Finn, in great surprise.

"It was foretold that I would catch the Salmon of All Knowledge," said Finegas. "But it was also foretold that only a man named Finn MacCool would eat the salmon. Since only you and I are here to eat the fish, I know your name must be Finn MacCool. The fish is yours to eat."

"Let us share it," urged Finn.

But Finegas shook his head. "The fish is for you alone," he said.

So Finn ate the Salmon of All Knowledge. With each bite, he felt his knowledge grow. Now, he knew why the stars shine and why the wind blows. He knew that he could do great deeds of magic, he could make mighty and marvelous poems, and he could compose awesomely beautiful music. And together with all these new things, he was still the fastest runner, the strongest man, and the most skillful warrior. Now, he was truly ready to go to Tara and see the High King.

The next day, Finn made his farewells to Finegas and set out. He came to Tara, the city of the High King, near sunset on Samhain Eve (which is now called

Halloween). He went to the High King's great hall and entered.

A huge feast was in progress, for this was the last day of the Celtic year and an important holiday. All the greatest warriors from all parts of the land had come to the feast given by the High King. Everyone was welcome, so Finn found an empty place at the table and sat down.

Samhain Eve was a very special time indeed. It was a time when magic was at its strongest, and strange things might happen. During the hours of darkness that followed sunset, the fairy mounds opened, allowing all kinds of evil creatures from the underworld—goblins, ghosts, and monsters—to walk the land!

Finn noticed that all through the feast, the High

King, whose name was Conn—Conn of the Hundred Battles—sat grim and silent. Finally, Conn stood up. The noise and laughter and loud talk stopped as men listened to hear what the High King had to say.

"Warriors of the Fianna," said Conn, "my wizards have given me grim and dreadful tidings. This night an evil creature from the Land of Darkness will come to destroy Tara! Aillen is its name, and it has the power to make men sleep, so that they cannot fight against it. It has the power to hurl spears of fire that will set Tara ablaze!" He looked around at all the warriors. "Is there any man here who will defend Tara against this dreadful doom?"

The men looked at him and they looked at one another. Then they hung their heads in shame. None of them felt able to do battle against this magical creature that could put men to sleep and hurl darts of fire.

But then, one man stood up. It was Finn MacCool.

"What reward would be given to the man who defends Tara from this evil one?" he asked.

"Whatever reward that man wants, I swear it will be given to him," answered Conn.

"I will defend Tara," said Finn.

"What is your name?" asked the High King.

"I am Finn, son of Cumhaill, of Clan Bascna," said Finn. A group of richly dressed men seated at a table near the king turned to stare when Finn gave his name. He knew they were the leaders of Clan Morna.

"You are the son of an old friend," said the High King. "I welcome you, and I thank you."

Then Finn turned and left the hall, for the sun had set and Aillen would soon appear. Finn walked through the city until he passed out of the gate and was beyond

the walls. There he stopped and faced the north. In his new-found wisdom, he knew that was the direction from which Aillen would come.

Finn carried no weapon, for he also knew that no ordinary weapon would be of any use against the dreadful Aillen. Having eaten the Salmon of All Knowledge, Finn knew of things that were going to happen before they happened. And he knew that he was going to be given a very special weapon to use against the monster.

Before long, he heard the sound of footsteps coming toward him. Turning, he saw that it was his father's old comrade, Fiacuil, the one who had taught him how to use both spear and sword. Fiacuil carried a spear. The point was wrapped in a leather bag that covered it completely.

"Finn," said Fiacuil, "I bring you a weapon to use

against Aillen. It is a weapon that your father himself captured from the Land of Darkness, from where Aillen comes. It is called the Poisonous Point!"

Finn knew that a weapon from the Land of Darkness would be magical and deadly indeed.

"Let me tell you how the Poisonous Point can help you," said the old warrior. "When Aillen comes, you will hear a harp playing the sweetest music ever heard. This is how he casts his spell of sleep. When drowsiness begins to steal over you, take the bag from off the spear's head. The sight, and the sound, and the smell of the Poisonous Point will keep you awake."

"I thank you, Fiacuil, man of Bascna, in my name and in my father's name," said Finn. The old warrior bowed, then he turned and made his way back into Tara.

No sooner had Fiacuil gone than Finn heard the notes of the magic harp. The night was as black as the blackest thing on earth, but moving out of the north was a shape that was even blacker. The only sound to be heard was the sweet music of the harp, but both the earth and the air shook from the force of the huge, heavy footsteps of Aillen. Slowly, surely, the dreadful monster strode toward Tara.

Suddenly, Finn felt drowsiness stealing over him. At once, he untied the cords that held the bag in place on the spearhead. Then he pulled off the bag and the Poisonous Point was revealed. It shone with a fiery red glow and made a sound like a shrill scream heard from a distance. A sharp, bitter, poisonous odor poured forth from it. The sight and sound and smell drove the drowsiness from Finn's mind.

From the formless black shape of Aillen there

suddenly shot forth a bolt of blue fire. It hissed through the air toward Tara, like a falling star that races through the night sky. But Finn MacCool had gained the knowledge of the world. He knew how to deal with magical fire. He lifted his hand. The fire splashed against it and died out in a shower of blue sparks.

Aillen stood frozen in astonishment. His spell of slumber should have everyone in Tara sleeping, yet here stood a man who was wide awake! His bolt of fire should have set Tara ablaze, but it had been snuffed out like a tiny candle flame!

Aillen knew that he had met his match, and more. Fear came over him, and he turned and fled.

But he could not outrun the man who had been

taught to run by the fleet forest deer. Behind him sped
Finn, drawing ever nearer. And in Finn's hand was the
terrible Poisonous Point. Aillen twisted and dodged, but
he could not trick the man who had been taught to leap
and dodge by the rabbits of the forest glade.

Back went Finn's arm, and with a heave he hurled

the Poisonous Point. It went into the body of Aillen and right on through, carrying the monster's life with it.

It was sunrise when Finn strode back into the High King's hall. Conn and all the warriors were there. They knew Finn had won the battle because Tara had not been burned down and they were still alive. When Finn entered the hall, they all stood and cheered him—even the men of Clan Morna.

"Name your reward, Finn MacCool," said the High King. "I wish to be captain of the Fianna, as was my father before me," said Finn.

"So shall it be," the High King said.

And so Finn MacCool got his wish and was made captain of the Fianna. And he became the greatest captain the Fianna ever had.

The Changing of the Sea People

Just off the very tip of South America there is a group of islands called Tierra del Fuego (tih EHR ah dehl foo AY goh). The name means "Land of Fire," but this is not a place of warmth. The islands are not very far from the South Pole, so they are cool in summer and cold and snowy in winter. Penguins come to the islands to lay eggs and rear their young. Seals abound in the water around the islands.

On some of the islands live the Yahgan Indian people. They make their living by fishing in the sea, from canoes. This story is one of their legends. No one knows how old the legend is, but the Yahgan people may have been telling it for thousands of years.

The Changing of the Sea People

The Yahgan people lived on a barren and gloomy island surrounded by the cold, gray sea. Life was hard for them. They spent most of their time just trying to find food. Each day the women and children roamed the beaches and waded in the shallows in search of shellfish. Each day the men went out onto the sea in flimsy canoes to catch fish.

In their canoes, the men could look down into the water and see the sea-bottom far below. Often, they saw dim figures moving about. These were the strange, dreadful creatures known as the Sea People, whose home was the bottom of the sea. The bodies of the Sea People were covered with dark fur. Their arms were long and thin, like the body of an eel. Their round heads had no noses.

The Yahgan men faced great danger from the Sea People. Sometimes huge crowds of the undersea creatures would rise to the surface to attack the men. They would surround one or two canoes, drag the men out, and then carry them down to the sea-bottom to eat them. There was nothing the Yahgan men could do to prevent this. The Sea People were too wild, savage, and strong for them.

But there came a day when a great hero was born among the Yahgan. He was named Naha, and when he grew up, he became known as Naha the Fighter. Naha had the strength of two men and feared nothing. If Naha were out fishing and a storm sprang up, with high, white waves that threatened to sink his canoe, he only grinned at the danger. If a huge, hungry shark began to circle his canoe, Naha merely laughed.

One day when Naha and the other men were out in their canoes, scores of the Sea People suddenly appeared. They surrounded the canoe of Naha the Fighter. When the creatures tried to seize him, Naha struck them with his fists. Such was his strength that each of the Sea People he struck was killed, and sank down into the water. The other creatures howled with rage and clustered about his canoe. Naha fought them off, grinning as he swung his powerful fists!

However, there were just too many of the creatures. More and more of them appeared. Two took the place of each one that Naha killed. By the scores they swarmed over his canoe. He no longer had room to swing his fists. Engulfed by a crowd of the creatures, he was dragged to the bottom of the sea!

As soon as he was on the sea-bottom, Naha broke free and began to fight again. Two, three, half a dozen of the Sea People were knocked lifeless to the sand. But more and more of them surrounded him. Some carried ropes made of seaweed with which to tie him up. Naha saw that he would soon be a helpless prisoner.

He turned and ran. In the distance was a rocky hill that rose upward. Naha thought that if he climbed the hill, he might reach the land above the sea. But the Sea People were close behind him!

When Naha reached the foot of the hill, he saw a large wooden door covering an opening into the rock. Somehow, he felt that the Sea People could not follow him through the door. He opened it and quickly stepped in.

He was in a gigantic cavern, so huge he could not see either its walls or ceiling. A glowing, sea-green light shone over everything. The sandy floor was not ordinary sand—it was glittering dust of gold and silver. Tall, twisted formations of pink, white, and red coral rose from the sand. Clouds of colorful fish were everywhere.

Filled with wonder, Naha began to walk through the marvelous cavern. Rounding a pillar of coral he came to a large open space. In the center of the space was a throne carved out of white coral. Upon the throne sat a woman. Her skin was as white as the coral, her hair was

as green as seaweed, and her eyes were the color of the
gray-green sea.

"Who are you, Man, and why are you here?" she
asked Naha, in a voice that made him think of waves
gently lapping against a shore.

"Woman of the Sea, my name is Naha," he told her.
"I am of the Yahgan people. I am here because the Sea
People attacked me, dragged me from my canoe, and
carried me down here to the sea-bottom. I fought,

killing many of them, and broke free. I ran until I found this place."

The sea woman was frowning slightly. "Why did the Sea People attack you?" she asked. "Had you done harm to them?"

"No, indeed!" Naha exclaimed. "As far back as the oldest Yahgan can remember, the Sea People have always attacked us. They use us for food! Life is bitter for my people, Sea Woman! They are often cold and hungry. But most terrible of all, they live in constant fear of the evil Sea People!"

The woman looked at him for a time, without saying anything. There was sadness in her eyes. Then she spoke again. "Would you like to free your people from the fear of the Sea People, Naha?"

"Of course I would, Sea Woman," he said. "But how can I?"

"There is only one way," she answered. "And that is to call the Great Cold that dwells beyond the stars. When the Great Cold comes, the Sea People will be changed so that your people will never have to fear them again."

"How may the Great Cold be called?" he asked.

"With this," she said, and held out a gleaming sea shell. "Blow into the shell, and the Great Cold will come."

Naha took the shell. The Sea Woman leaned forward and put her hand on his shoulder. "But listen well to me, Naha," she said, looking into his eyes. "Your people must leave the island before the Great Cold is called! If they are there when it arrives, they will die! Only one can stay behind—the one who blows the shell. That one will die so that the Yahgan may live!"

"I understand," said Naha, softly.

"Then, farewell," she said, sadly. She pointed into the distance. "Go that way. In time, you will find yourself above the sea."

Naha turned and strode off. For a long time he walked through the glowing, sea-green light. Finally, the light faded to gray and Naha saw clouds overhead. The sand beneath his feet was no longer gold and silver—it was ordinary sand. He was back on the island.

Naha made his way to the village of his people. They were wild with joy to see him, for they had thought he was dead. They listened with wonder to his story. They stared with awe at the gleaming sea shell.

"So, you must make ready now," Naha told them. "Load your possessions into your canoes. Paddle northward until you can no longer see our land. When you are safely gone, I will summon the Great Cold. Within three days time, its work will be done and you can return."

The people looked at one another. One of them spoke. "Come with us, Naha," he said. "Be our leader. Please! Someone else will blow the shell."

"I will blow it," said an old man. "It does not matter if I die. Go with the people and be their leader, Naha!"

Many others offered to blow the shell. Naha smiled proudly at them, but he shook his head. "It was given to me," he said. "I am the one who must blow the shell and bring the Great Cold."

He finally got everyone to agree. They loaded their few belongings into their canoes and sadly said their farewells. Silently, they climbed into the canoes and began to paddle away.

Naha stood on the beach and watched them until

they were out of sight. Then he turned and walked slowly toward the center of the island. He climbed to the top of a small hill. He gazed about at the gray sea rolling in toward the land and at the gray sky overhead. Then he lifted the sea shell to his lips and blew into it.

A clear, high, loud note sang out from the shell. It seemed to reach out to all parts of the land, sea, and sky. From the island, a great cloud of birds arose and quickly went winging out of sight. Out in the sea, whales and dolphins turned and headed away from the island. Warned by the call of the sea shell, all these creatures sought to escape the coming of the Great Cold.

But from out of the water around the island came hundreds of the furry, noseless Sea People. Silently, with staring eyes, they waded up onto the beaches. For them, the sound of the shell was like a magnet, drawing them to the island.

At that moment, the Great Cold reached out from beyond the stars.

There was a sound like a thunderclap, and the surface of the sea around the island turned to green, glittering ice. On the island, every rock and boulder turned white with frost. A great shrieking wind scattered white flakes of snow in the air. And the air grew bone-cracking, fire-freezing cold!

The bodies of the Sea People began to shrink and shrivel from the cold. Their long arms and their legs became flippers. They could no longer stand nor walk. They lay on the icy beaches, making frightened barking noises. They had become the kind of animal we call seals!

Three days later, the Yahgan people returned to their

island. The Great Cold had departed. Once again, flocks
of gulls wheeled and soared over the shore. Dolphins
raced and leaped in the sea nearby.

There were also many furry seals swimming in the
water and sunning themselves on the rocky beaches.
But if a man, woman, or child came near them, they
immediately fled in fear. Never again would the Yahgan
have to be afraid of the Sea People!

The Yahgan people sorrowfully searched for the body
of Naha. But they never found him. All they found were
broken fragments of the sea shell with which he had
called the Great Cold from beyond the stars.

The Prince and the Evil Sorcerer

The hero, the villain, and most of the other people
in this tale were real people. Many of the things that
take place in the tale really did happen. They
happened more than seven hundred years ago, in the
part of Africa that is now the nation of Mali.

For hundreds of years, the storytellers of Mali,
called *griots* (GREE ohs), have told this tale.
However, as storytellers often do, they sometimes
changed things a bit. For one thing, they put a lot of
magical happenings into the story. So what was
actually history has been turned into legend—a tale
full of magic as well as heroic deeds.

161

The Prince and the Evil Sorcerer

In the center of the city of Sosso, in West Africa, there rose a seven-story tower. At the top of the tower was a secret room. It was a place of evil magic! In the middle of the room stood a large clay bowl filled with water, in which a huge snake lay coiled. In a circle around the bowl were nine human skulls. On a stool lay a robe made of human skins.

In this room, Sumanguru the Sorcerer, king of Sosso and lands beyond, cast his spells. The most powerful of all kings was Sumanguru—and the most wicked of all men!

It was said that he had made a bargain with Evil, and had been given power over jinns, afreets, and other dreadful demons. The huge snake in his magic room was one of these demons. With their help, Sumanguru had conquered nine nearby kingdoms. The nine skulls in his tower room were the heads of the defeated kings of those kingdoms. The robe, which he often wore, was made from their skins!

The people of the conquered lands lived in fear and

misery, for Sumanguru ruled them harshly. He was without pity and without mercy. He delighted in death and torture!

One of the lands conquered by Sumanguru was the land of Kangaba. But many of the people of Kangaba refused to be ruled by the wicked sorcerer. They left their towns and went into the forest to hide. They were determined to make war against Sumanguru and drive him from their land. But could they win against his magic? They called upon their own magicians to look into the future and see.

The magicians drummed and chanted. They cast the twelve magic snail shells on the ground and studied the patterns the shells made. Every magician said the same thing: "Kangaba will be saved by its true king, 'The Man with Two Names.'"

The wise men of Kangaba looked at one another and

nodded. "The Man with Two Names" was the youngest
son of their great king, Nare Maghan, who had died
eight years ago. The son had been called Maridiata, or
Lion-Prince, when he was born. But as a little child, he
had very weak legs. Unable to walk, he crawled about,
constantly stealing food. Because of this, people called
him Sundiata, or Thief-Lion. And so it was that he had
two names.

But where was Sundiata? No one knew. When King
Nare Maghan had died, his eldest son, Dankaran
Touman, had become king. Dankaran Touman and
Sundiata did not have the same mother, and
Dankaran's mother hated Sundiata. Even though
Sundiata was only ten years old, she worried that he
would take the throne from her son. Fearing that
Dankaran's mother would have Sundiata killed,
Sundiata's mother had taken him and his sisters away.
No one knew where they had gone.

Men and women were sent to search for Sundiata.
They traveled to distant lands, hoping to find the young
prince and bring him back to lead the fight against
Sumanguru.

Two of the men came to a city called Mema. They
pretended to be merchants, selling leaves of the monkey
bread tree and other spices from Kangaba. Such things
were unknown in Mema, and most people paid no
attention to them. But the men thought that if anyone
from Kangaba were living in Mema, this food from their
homeland would attract their attention.

Several days passed. Then a young girl stopped to
look at the spices. "Cola nuts," she exclaimed in delight.
"And monkey bread leaves! I haven't seen any of these
since I was a little girl in Kangaba!"

"Do you have a brother?" asked one of the men, hopefully.

"Why, yes," she said, in surprise. "His name is Sundiata."

"Will you take us to him?" said the man. "We have come all the way from Kangaba in search of him!"

So Sundiata's sister took them to her home. There, they met Sundiata's mother, his other sister, and Sundiata himself. He was now eighteen years old—a tall, sturdy young man. During the years he had lived in Mema, he had become a skillful hunter and a courageous warrior in the service of Moussa Tounkara, king of Mema. And the king, who had no sons, had come to love Sundiata as if he were his own son.

"What news do you bring from Kangaba?" asked Sundiata's mother.

"The news is sorrowful," said one of the men. "Sumanguru, the powerful king of Sosso, has conquered

our land. His rule is harsh and cruel. The people are
ready to rise up and fight for their freedom, but they
have no leader." He looked at Sundiata. "The magicians
have said that you, Sundiata, will be our leader, that
you will free us from the misery of Sumanguru's rule.
We hail you as the new king of Kangaba! We ask that
you return with us. The people await you!"

Sundiata was not surprised. He had long believed that
someday he would return to Kangaba and become king.
"I will go with you," he told the men. "We will leave in
the morning."

He went to say good-by to Moussa Tounkara, the
king of Mema. The old man was sorry to see him go.

But he gave Sundiata half of the army of Mema to help
him win his kingdom from the evil sorcerer, Sumanguru.
The next morning, with the soldiers of Mema riding
behind him, Sundiata rode toward Kangaba.

That same morning, in the room of magic at the top
of the seven-story tower in Sosso, Sumanguru was
weaving a spell. The room was thick with curling smoke
that seemed to fill the air with strange whispers! The
great snake lifted its head up out of the bowl and gazed
at Sumanguru with glowing green eyes.

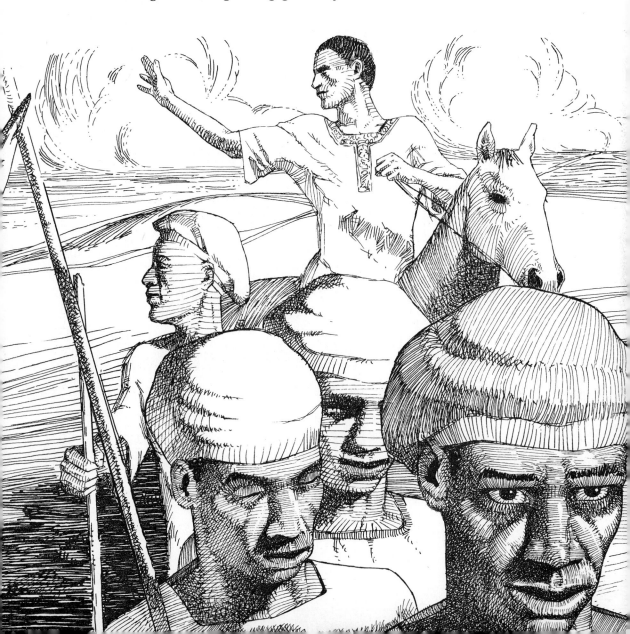

"Tell me, O Wise One, who comes against me?" asked Sumanguru.

"Sundiata, the rightful king of Kangaba," answered the snake in a voice like a soft, sighing wind. "He comes from Mema, with an army of horsemen!"

Thus, by means of magic, Sumanguru learned of the coming of Sundiata. He began to assemble a great army. He intended to meet the young king in battle and destroy him!

But as Sundiata rode toward Kangaba, hundreds of warriors from cities and towns that had been conquered by Sumanguru came to join him—archers from Tabon, the City of the Iron Gate, foot soldiers and horsemen from Wagadou, and many, many others. The army of Sundiata grew until it was as large and as powerful as the army of Sumanguru.

Sumanguru marched his army to a narrow valley that lay in the path of Sundiata's army. The sorcerer spread his men across the valley and waited. At noon, when the sun was straight overhead, the army of Sundiata appeared.

Sundiata gazed upon his enemy's army and quickly made his plans. He had all his soldiers form a great square, with the horsemen in front and row upon row of archers behind them. Then Sundiata gave the signal. War horns blared and war drums thundered.

Slowly, Sundiata's horsemen rode into the valley. As they did, the archers raised their bows and sent a rain of arrows over the heads of the horsemen. The clouds of arrows flying through the air blocked out the sun and put the valley in shade. Hundreds upon hundreds of arrows hissed down upon the warriors of Sosso and slew them by the score.

Then the archers halted their fire. With Sundiata at their head, the horsemen charged!

All afternoon the battle raged. Sundiata seemed to be everywhere at once. Wherever he was needed to give courage to his men, he appeared. His sword flashed like a bolt of lightning.

Suddenly Sundiata caught sight of Sumanguru. His enemy was mounted on a splendid black horse. With a shout of triumph, Sundiata rode toward the sorcerer. With all his might, he flung his spear at Sumanguru's chest!

But the spear bounced off the sorcerer as if he were made of iron! Sumanguru smiled—and, to Sundiata's amazement, suddenly disappeared!

The sun was setting now. Slowly, the army of Sosso began to draw back out of the valley. The men of Sundiata's army were simply too worn out to follow them. The battle was clearly a victory for Sundiata and his men. The soldiers began to rejoice and celebrate.

But Sundiata did not rejoice. He was worried and uncertain. A number of magicians had become part of his army, so he called them all together for a meeting.

"How can I overcome the magic of Sumanguru?" he asked. "If I am to free the people he has conquered, I must slay him. But how can I slay a man who cannot be harmed by a sharp spear? How can I slay a man who can vanish before my eyes?"

The magicians could not answer him. But at that moment, a soldier came up to Sundiata. "Oh king," he said, "a woman has come to the army, looking for you. Her name is Nana Triban. She says she can tell you how to slay Sumanguru!"

Sundiata's eyes lit up with gladness. He and Nana

Triban had been good friends when they were children. He would be glad to see her. "Bring her to me," he told the soldier.

A short time later the man returned with Nana Triban. She was a pretty girl, about the same age as Sundiata.

"It is good to see you, friend of my childhood," smiled Sundiata. "How have things been for you?"

"My life has been hard, Sundiata," she told him. "When Sumanguru conquered our land, he took me to be one of his wives." She shivered. "I was frightened, for he is an evil man and his eyes are like the eyes of a snake! But he liked me, and told me some of his secrets of magic. I know how he can be killed, Sundiata! When he left Sosso to fight you, I escaped and came to tell you how to destroy him!"

"How?" Sundiata asked, eagerly.

"He cannot be killed with iron or stone," she said, "which is why your spear was useless. He fears only one thing—the claw of a rooster!"

Sundiata was overjoyed. Now that he had Sumanguru's secret, he felt sure he could destroy the wicked sorcerer. He and Nana Triban joined the soldiers in the great victory feast.

Late that night, when all the others were sleeping, Sundiata walked by himself in the moonlight. He sat down beneath a baobab tree to consider his plans. An owl came skimming through the air and alighted on a branch of the tree. Sundiata felt a cold chill settle over his body. He knew that the owl was a creature of magic.

"Young prince," said the owl, in the voice of a man, "I am Sumanguru! Go back to Mema in peace and I shall spare you. But if you put yourself against me, I shall destroy you! I am the king of these lands. I am the tallest tree in the forest. I look down upon all others!"

"I fear you not, Sumanguru," answered Sundiata, gazing straight into the owl's glowing eyes. "If you want peace, give up the lands you have stolen and stay in Sosso. If you put yourself against me, I will slay you! For I am the *true* king of these lands! I am the ax that can chop down the tree!"

"Foolish child, you are doomed!" said the owl, and flew away.

The next morning, Sundiata went to one of his soldiers who was known to be a skillful maker of arrows. He had the man make a very special arrow for him. Then he called his army together and set out toward Sosso—the city of Sumanguru.

But on the road to Sosso stood the little village of

Kirina. And it was there that Sumanguru waited with his army, to stop Sundiata from reaching Sosso.

It was just after sunrise when the two armies met. All morning long the howl of war horns, the thud of drums, the thunder of charging horses, and the shouts of warriors filled the air. Once again Sundiata rode from place to place, wherever he was needed to help his soldiers. But always he watched for Sumanguru.

Things were not going well for Sundiata's army. When his men tried to move forward, they often found a fierce and terrible wind pushing against them so that they could hardly move. Sundiata realized that Sumanguru was using magic against his men. Desperately, he searched the field of battle for the sorcerer.

At last he saw him. Quickly Sundiata pulled the special arrow from his quiver. He fitted the arrow to his bowstring, pulled the bowstring back to his shoulder, and shot. Up, up soared the arrow in a great curve. Down, down it sped toward its target. It struck Sumanguru in the arm.

It was not a serious wound, but when Sumanguru pulled out the arrow, he stared at it in horror. Then he let out a long, wailing shriek that rang across the battlefield. The sharp arrowhead was made from the claw of a rooster! This was the secret Nana Triban had told to Sundiata—the one thing that Sumanguru feared, the one thing that could destroy him. For when he was struck by the rooster claw, he lost all his powers of magic!

Sumanguru knew that he was beaten. He turned his horse and galloped from the field. Seeing him flee, the men of Sosso lost their courage. They threw down their

weapons and ran in fear. The battle was over. The men
of Sundiata had won!

No one ever saw Sumanguru again. Sundiata led his
men to Sosso and captured the city. He had the
seven-story tower torn down and everything in the room
of magic destroyed.

Thus did Sundiata set free all the people who had
lived in misery under Sumanguru's rule. And so it was
that Sundiata became king of a vast land that had once
been many small kingdoms. This land became known as
Mali, the name it has kept to this day—a name that
means "where the king lives."

The Brave Coward

This is a legend of the Sioux Indian people of North America. It is probably several thousand years old.

The Sioux called themselves *Dakota* or *Lakota,* meaning "Allies," because there were many separate groups. The Sioux admired bravery, but they knew that fearless people were not the only ones who were brave. A person could be very frightened and still be brave. The hero of this tale is just such a person.

The Brave Coward

In the land of the Dakota people there was a lake, and on the lake there was an island. Upon the island lived a tribe whose chief was a man known as Red Head.

Red Head was an evil man and a powerful sorcerer. He had slain many a Dakota with magic, and the Dakotas were in terror of him. It was the great wish and dream of every young Dakota brave to kill Red Head. The man who could do that would be the greatest of all warriors. But any man who tried to get near the wicked magician was always slain himself!

In one Dakota village there lived a hunter who had a wife and young son. One evening, the hunter asked his son to bring some water from the nearby river. But the son refused, saying that it was dark and he was afraid to go through the woods to the river.

"If you are afraid of mere darkness, *you* will never be the one to slay Red Head," said his father, scornfully.

This made the young man feel greatly ashamed. He felt he could no longer stay with his parents. The next

morning at sunrise, before his father or mother were
awake, he left his father's lodge.

He did not know where he should go, so he decided to
shoot an arrow into the air and follow wherever it went.
The arrow sailed far up into the sky and curved down
out of sight into the forest. The young man followed
after it. Each day, for the next four days, he did this
again. But by the morning of the fifth day, all his
arrows were gone.

The young man wandered on through the forest. He
had used up all his food, and by nightfall he was very
hungry. But without any arrows he could not do any
hunting. He lay down upon the ground to sleep and
forget his hunger.

He had not been lying there long when he heard a

strange sound. He stood up to see what was causing it
and beheld a little old woman walking toward him. She
was using a stick as a cane, and the stick was decorated
with the feet and bills of many kinds of birds. Each
time the stick touched the ground, all the bills broke
into chirps and twitters for a moment. This was the odd
noise that had startled the young man.

He now became dreadfully afraid, for he recognized
the old woman. She was a terrible witch, known as
Little-Old-Woman-Who-Makes-Trouble. He looked
around for a hiding place, but it was too late. The old
woman came straight to him.

"Don't be afraid of me," she said. "I've been watching
you ever since you left your father's lodge. I want to
help you, and be your friend. I know you think that
you'll never be a brave warrior, but you will be. I'll see
to it!"

The young man was overjoyed to hear her words.
When she invited him to come to her lodge for
something to eat, he gladly went with her.

The next morning, Little-Old-Woman-Who-Makes-
Trouble said, "Now I will make the magic that will
make it possible for you to become the Dakota warrior
who will slay Red Head!"

Taking her comb, she ran it several times through his
hair. His short hair suddenly grew long, like the hair of
a maiden. Next, the old woman painted his face so that
he looked like a beautiful girl. Then she gave him girl's
clothing to put on. Finally, she handed him a bowl
made of shining metal, and a blade of the tough,
sharp-edged grass known as knife grass.

"Come with me," she said.

The young man, who now looked like a very pretty

young girl, followed her to the shore of a lake. She pointed across the lake toward a distant island.

"That is the island of Red Head and his tribe," she said. "He and his warriors will soon be coming from there, in their canoes. You must walk about here, on the shore, and let them see you. The way you look, and the spell of the shining bowl, will make them all think you are a beautiful girl. They will all want to marry you. Tell Red Head that you agree to marry him!

"Red Head will take you back to the island in his canoe," the old woman went on. "When night comes, you must get him to take a walk with you, in the darkness. Somehow, you must manage to slide the blade of knife grass across his throat. I have put a spell upon it, so that it will cut off his head! You must swim back here with the head—and you will be the greatest of all Dakota braves!"

The young man was badly frightened at the thought of risking his life trying to do all this. But he remembered how scornfully his father had looked at him and spoken to him, and this made him feel ashamed again. He decided he must try to follow the old woman's plan no matter how frightened he was, or else he would always be ashamed of himself!

The old woman went back to her lodge, and the young man began to walk back and forth on the shore. Before long, he saw many canoes coming toward him across the lake. His heart started to beat fast from fright, but he forced himself to keep on walking slowly and calmly.

The men pulled their canoes up onto the shore and then came crowding around the young man. The old woman's magic spell was working upon them. "Oh, what a beautiful maiden," exclaimed one. "Be my wife, pretty one," begged another.

Then a tall man pushed his way forward from among them all. His face was painted red, and his hair was dyed red, with red feathers twisted into it. The young man knew this must be the dreaded wizard, Red Head!

"Marry me, you most beautiful of all girls," he said. "I will give you gifts. You will never have to work!"

"I will marry you, Red Head," said the young man. He made his voice sound high and soft, like that of a young girl.

"Enter my canoe," said Red Head, joyfully. "I shall take you to my island, where we shall have a great feast. Tonight, we shall be married!"

The young man started to get into the canoe. However, to his dismay, he saw that the framework of the canoe was formed out of live rattlesnakes, which began to hiss and rattle at him! But Red Head spoke to them and they became quiet.

Red Head paddled the canoe swiftly to the island, followed by all his warriors in their canoes. Reaching the island, everyone hurried to Red Head's lodge, where he told his mother to quickly prepare food for a huge wedding feast.

While the feast was taking place, Red Head's mother stared and stared at the young man. The magic did not seem to be working on her. The more she looked, the more it seemed to her that this "girl" her son wanted to marry was really a man!

"What do you know about this person?" she asked Red Head.

"She is the most beautiful girl I ever saw," said Red Head, with a happy smile.

"I do not think this person is a girl," said his mother. "I think this person is a man."

"How can you say such a thing?" asked Red Head, angrily. "I will not listen to such foolishness!"

It was night by now, and the young man saw his chance to get Red Head to go off with him, alone, as Little-Old-Woman-Who-Makes-Trouble had suggested. He stood up. "I have been insulted," he said in an angry voice. "I cannot marry a man whose mother thinks so poorly of me!" He walked out of the lodge.

As he hoped, Red Head came hurrying after him. "Please don't leave," cried Red Head. "Come back and marry me!"

"Your mother was very rude to me," said the young man, and kept on walking. "I could never live in the same lodge with her."

"I'll send her away to live somewhere else," declared Red Head, following after him. "I'll beat her if you wish! Please don't leave."

They had now reached the beach, so the young man stopped. He looked around. They were all alone in the darkness. Carefully, so that Red Head wouldn't notice, he slid the blade of knife grass out from where he had hidden it in the dress he was wearing.

"Oh! Look there!" he suddenly cried, and pointed at the sky.

Red Head lifted his head to look up. Quickly, the young man reached out and slashed the blade of grass across Red Head's throat. It was as if the blade of grass were a sharp sword. It sliced Red Head's head right off his body! The wicked magician was no more!

Holding the head by the hair, the young man quickly waded into the water and swam back across the lake.

Reaching the far shore, he hurried to the lodge of
Little-Old-Woman-Who-Makes-Trouble. "I'm back," he
called.

"So you are," said she, grinning. "And I see you were
successful. Now no one can ever say you're not brave!"

"I wasn't brave at all," he said, sounding ashamed. "I
was frightened every moment!"

"But that's what true bravery *is*, foolish boy," the old
woman chuckled. "It is doing what you have to do, even
though you are so frightened you'd rather run away!"

The next morning, after thanking the old woman for
all her help, the young man, who now looked like
himself again, set out to return to his village. When he
got there, he went straight to his parents' lodge. He
held the head of Red Head behind his back so that it
was hidden. He found his parents sitting side by side

with their heads down, grieving because they thought
he had gone away forever.

"Son, you have returned," cried his mother, joyfully.

"I know you left because my words made you
ashamed," said his father. "I am sorry I hinted that you
were a coward."

"Do not be sorry, for I am a coward," said the young
man. "But I have learned how to be brave even though
I am a coward!"

He then showed them the head of Red Head and told
them of what had happened. News of what he had done
quickly spread throughout the village, and was carried
to other villages. Soon the young man was known
throughout the entire Dakota tribe as the bravest of all
warriors. And, in time, he became a great and famous
chief.

The Monster in the Maze

This story from ancient Greece is at least twenty-five hundred years old. When this story was first told, Greece was called Hellas. At that time, the land was divided into many small communities called city-states. Nearly every city-state had tales about its favorite hero. The story of the monster in the maze is one of the tales about Theseus (THEE see uhs or THEE soos), the greatest of all the heroes of the city-state of Athens.

The Monster in the Maze

In olden times, the people of Athens and the
people of Crete, an island in the Mediterranean Sea,
fought a bloody and bitter war. Athens was defeated.

Minos, the king of Crete, wanted to humble the
Athenians and make them remember their defeat. To do
this, he ordered that they make a yearly sacrifice of
seven young men and seven young maidens. The
fourteen young people were to be sent to Crete. There,
they would be sacrificed to a terrifying monster known
as the Minotaur.

The Minotaur was a strange creature, half man and
half bull. Huge, tremendously strong, and very fierce,
the Minotaur was kept in a vast building called the
Labyrinth. The Labyrinth was a maze, with winding,
crisscrossing passageways and only one entrance. Those
who entered could not possibly find their way out. Each
year, the fourteen young Athenians were forced to go
into the Labyrinth. There they wandered about until
they encountered the Minotaur prowling through the
darkness in search of its prey.

Now it so happened that Aegeus, the king of Athens, had a son who did not live in the city. The boy's name was Theseus. He had been born in a place far from Athens, where he had spent the first part of his life. But at the age of sixteen, Theseus set out for Athens to join his father at last.

It was a long and dangerous journey, but Theseus was tremendously strong and he had great courage. He had also sworn to help people whenever he could. Theseus had many adventures on his way to Athens. He fought and killed a giant hog that was destroying the crops and fields of farmers. He fought and punished a number of evil bandits who robbed and tortured people. Thus, when he reached Athens, he was welcomed as a hero. The people rejoiced to see him.

But while the Athenians were singing and cheering to honor him, Theseus saw one group of people who stood sad and silent, or wept with grief. "Why are those people grieving, Father?" he asked the king.

"They weep for their children, for they shall never see them again." King Aegeus answered sadly. "They are the parents of the fourteen young Athenians who have been chosen as sacrifices to the Minotaur."

The face of Theseus grew grim and his eyes darkened with anger. "Father," he said, "I am going to take the place of one of the young men who was picked to go to Crete. I shall be one of those sent to be sacrificed to the Minotaur!"

"What are you saying, Theseus?" gasped the king. "You will be going to your death!"

Theseus shook his head. "I shall not be the one to

die," said he. "I intend to slay the Minotaur and free
the young people of Athens from this terrible fear they
must face each year!"

"Theseus, you are strong and brave, but you may not
be a match for the terrible Minotaur," said his father.
"And even if you could kill the creature, how would you
then get out of the Labyrinth, from which there is no
escape?"

"There must be a way. I shall find it," said Theseus.
"I feel that the gods will help me, Father."

Despite all his father's pleas, Theseus was determined
to go. The next day, when the black-sailed ship taking
the fourteen young people to Crete left Athens, Theseus
was on it.

The ship sped over the dark, sparkling sea toward
Crete. When they arrived, the cruel, black-bearded King

Minos stood on the shore with a group of people and soldiers. Beside him stood the beautiful Ariadne, his daughter, who was the same age as Theseus.

There was sadness in the eyes of Ariadne as she watched the Athenians come off the ship. It seemed dreadful to her that these girls and boys, young and full of life just as she was, were doomed to be slain and devoured by the Minotaur.

As Theseus marched off the ship with the other Athenians, he caught sight of the beautiful, dark-haired Ariadne. He stopped short and stared at her. Ariadne could only stare back at him. They had fallen in love at first sight.

It was late in the day when the ship had arrived, and twilight now began to steal over the island of Crete. King Minos gave orders to put the Athenians into separate dungeons for the night. The next day, they would be sent into the Labyrinth.

When the sky turned black and the silver moon rose, Ariadne slipped out of her room in the palace. She could not bear to think that Theseus would die the next day. She had decided to help him and the other Athenians escape—even though she would face the terrible anger of her father and all the people of Crete. Silently, she stole down to the dark dungeon where Theseus lay resting.

"Theseus," she whispered, "I cannot bear to think of the horrible Minotaur killing you. I have come to help you and the others escape."

"Princess, I thank you with all my heart," said Theseus. "But I cannot run away. I have come to Crete to slay the Minotaur so that no Athenian boy or girl will ever again have to fear it!"

"I fear for you, Theseus," said Ariadne, anxiously. "The Minotaur is huge and fierce."

"I shall slay it," said Theseus. "It is not the Minotaur I fear, it is the Labyrinth. After I slay the creature, how can I escape from the maze?"

Now it happened that Ariadne knew how it was possible to escape from the Labyrinth! The trick had been revealed to her by the very man who had built the maze. She ran quickly back to her room. In a short time she returned with a large ball of yarn and the key to Theseus' dungeon.

"Theseus, if you must go into the Labyrinth, fasten the end of this yarn near the entrance," she told him. "Unwind the yarn as you go through the maze. When you want to come out, just follow the trail of yarn."

Theseus was overjoyed. Ariadne let him out of the dungeon, and together they stole through the moonlight to the Labyrinth.

"Wait here for me," whispered Theseus. "When I get back, we shall free the others and return to the ship that brought us here. You must come with us, Ariadne. It will not be safe for you here. Your father's rage will be terrible when he discovers that you are the one who helped us. Will you come back to Athens with me, and be my wife?"

"I will," she whispered.

They said farewell to each other. Then Theseus fastened the end of the yarn beneath a heavy rock and entered the Labyrinth.

It was as black as a moonless midnight inside. Theseus paused for a moment so that his eyes might get used to the darkness. Then he began to move through the maze, unwinding the yarn as he went.

The narrow, winding passageway seemed to go on and on without end. Every so often it branched out into two or even three new passageways. Then Theseus would have to decide which to take. Sometimes he found himself passing through thick cobwebs and knew he must be in a place where no one had been for years. He heard the squeaks of scurrying rats and the rustle of bats flying past his head. Once or twice he passed piles of human bones.

On and on Theseus went, with the ball of yarn growing ever smaller. Then he stopped. He had heard a sound. Something was moving through the passageway toward him, breathing loudly and walking with heavy footsteps. In the darkness he saw the gleam of two red eyes. He could barely make out a huge figure with the body of a man and the horned head of a bull. It was the Minotaur!

With a bellow of rage, the creature lowered its head

and charged. Theseus sprang to meet it. In the darkness
they began to wrestle, each struggling to slay the other!

Outside the Labyrinth, Ariadne waited in the
moonlight. At times she thought she heard a noise deep
within the Labyrinth—a noise that sounded like the
bellowing of a bull. She prayed that Theseus would
return safely to her.

Suddenly she heard footsteps inside the Labyrinth.
They were coming toward the entrance! Her heart
began to beat wildly. She prayed that it was Theseus.
But, what if it were the Minotaur!

The footsteps grew louder. A figure stepped out of
the Labyrinth. Ariadne gave a sob of joy. It was
Theseus.

"I have slain the Minotaur," he said.

They hurried to the dungeons to release the young
Athenians. Then Theseus, Ariadne, and the others ran
to the beach, where they boarded the ship that had
brought them from Athens. Soon they were heading out
to sea, leaving Crete behind. Because of Theseus'
bravery in fighting the horrible Minotaur, and Ariadne's
bravery in helping him, no other young Athenian would
ever again have to leave grieving parents and be
sacrificed to the monster in the maze.

The Green Knight's Challenge

The story of the Green Knight and the man named
Gawain was first written as a poem about six
hundred years ago in England. But people had
probably been telling the story for hundreds of years
before that. Gawain was the hero in a number of
very old stories. Some of the stories about him got
mixed in with stories about King Arthur and his
Knights of the Round Table. In time, Gawain
became Sir Gawain—one of Arthur's knights.

The story of Sir Gawain and the Green Knight,
like many stories of King Arthur's knights, shows
what people of long ago thought a knight should
be—a man who kept his word, no matter how
difficult this might be.

The Green Knight's Challenge

t was New Year's Day. At Camelot Castle, King Arthur of Britain was holding a great feast. All his warriors, the Knights of the Round Table, were gathered together. The great hall of the castle was bright with the glow of hundreds of candles. It rang with happy laughter and the sound of many voices. Outside, winter lay upon the land, but within was warmth and joy.

Then, suddenly, a cold wind seemed to sigh through the great room. It was as if the breath of winter had blown into the castle. The talk and laughter died away. The knights and ladies stared toward the far end of the hall. A strange figure had entered and stood there.

It was a green man! His head was uncovered, so they could see that his skin was as green as summer's grass. His hair and beard were the color of oak leaves. He was clad in armor as green and shiny as a holly leaf.

For many moments, the Green Knight stood looking at the crowd of knights and ladies seated at the table. They stared back at him. No one made a sound. Then, the Green Knight spoke.

"I have come to deliver a challenge to the Knights of
the Round Table," he said. His voice was strong and
deep.

King Arthur's knights glanced at one another. Their
duty was to keep the land peaceful and happy. To do
this, they often had to fight wicked knights, sorcerers,
and evil creatures. Thus, they were all fine fighters. If
this strange green knight wanted combat, any one of
Arthur's knights was ready to meet him!

The Green Knight spoke again. "This is my
challenge," he said. "Any one of you can try to strike
off my head with a single blow of your sword. But if I
survive that blow, you must come to me a year from
today—and let me strike a blow at you in return!"

Again the knights looked at one another. But now
they were not so sure of themselves. It seemed to them
that the Green Knight must be protected by magic if he

would offer to let someone try to cut off his head. But Arthur's knights had no such magic to protect them. They dared not accept this challenge!

The Green Knight stood, calmly waiting. The room stayed silent. After a time, the green man smiled, scornfully.

"Will no one accept my challenge?" he asked. "What is so difficult about cutting off a man's head? I promise you, I will not fight."

The knights shifted their feet and muttered. But no one answered him.

The Green Knight's smile grew more scornful. "It is said that the knights of King Arthur are all brave men," he said. "But that may not be true. You do not seem very brave to me!"

King Arthur scowled. It angered him greatly to hear

someone say that his warriors were not brave. But Arthur could see that the Green Knight was trying to trick them all. He hoped that none of his men would be so angry as to accept the challenge.

The Green Knight threw back his head and laughed. "Nay, it seems the Knights of the Round Table are not brave after all," he taunted. "They are naught but cowards!"

One of Arthur's knights was a sturdy, golden-haired, blue-eyed young man named Gawain. Sir Gawain was tremendously proud to be a Knight of the Round Table. He had fought in many combats and risked his life many times. To be called a coward was more than he could bear. He rose to his feet. "I accept your challenge!" he shouted.

King Arthur groaned. "Nay, Gawain! It is a trap for you!"

"Do you pledge that if I survive your blow you will come to me in a year's time and take a blow from me?" demanded the Green Knight.

"Nay, Gawain, nay!" cried Arthur and several of the other knights.

But, proudly, Gawain said, "I give my pledge."

"Then come and strike your blow," said the Green Knight. He knelt down and bent his head so that Gawain might strike his blow more easily.

Gawain drew his sword. He left his place at the table and walked to where the Green Knight knelt. He hoped that the knight would quickly withdraw the challenge, or admit that it was a trick. He did not want to kill the man.

But the Green Knight did not move. Gawain saw that he would have to go through with this. He would have to strike the man with his full strength. With his legs spread, he stood over the kneeling man. He raised the sword high over his head. There was a flash and a hiss as he brought it swiftly down. The knights and ladies gasped as the blade sliced through the Green Knight's neck! His head fell to the floor!

But the Green Knight was not dead! His arms stretched out and picked up his head! Slowly, he stood up and held his head so that it faced Gawain.

"You have given your pledge, Sir Gawain," said the head. "One year from today, be at the Green Chapel. I will meet you there and strike my blow!"

Then still holding his head before him, the Green Knight turned and walked from the hall. In astonished silence, Gawain and all the others watched him go.

After a time, Gawain slowly walked back to his place at the table. The knights and ladies seated near him looked at him sadly. They felt he had given his life away. Gawain, too, realized how foolish he had been to accept the Green Knight's challenge. He had been tricked into letting the Green Knight kill him a year from now!

Winter passed and spring came. The trees put on bright coats of pink, white, and green. Grass and flowers began to spring up across the land. As Gawain looked at all the fresh beauty, he remembered that this would be the last spring he would ever see!

Summer came. It was a happy time for most people—a time of warm, pleasant days. But Gawain, thinking of what was to happen at the end of the year, was often sad.

Summer slipped into autumn. The trees put on coats of red, yellow, and orange. Many of them were filled to bursting with fruit or nuts. Farmers harvested their fields of golden grain. This, too, was a happy time, and a time of plenty. But Gawain stayed away from the harvest feasts and merriment. He could no longer be cheerful.

Autumn turned into winter, and the first snow fell. Gawain went to King Arthur.

"Sire, I bid you farewell," he said. "It is a long journey to the Green Chapel, and I must set out in a few days if I am to arrive by New Year's Day."

"Do not go, Gawain," urged the king. "It will mean your death! You need not keep your pledge. You were tricked by that foul sorcerer! I say that he has no claim on you!"

But Gawain shook his head. "I must go, Sire," he

said, firmly. "It matters not that it was a trick. I gave
my pledge, and I must keep it. If I do not, I will be
dishonored as a knight."

Gawain's friends also tried to keep him from going.
But he told them the same thing he had told the king.
"I gave my word. I must keep it."

On a bleak day in November, Gawain set out. He had
polished his armor until it sparkled, and he rode his
finest war horse, Gringolet.

Gawain did not know exactly where the Green Chapel
was, only that it lay far to the south. Day after day, he
made his way across the land. Only at night did he stop
to rest. Sometimes he found an inn or a monastery
where he had supper and spent the night. But most
often he slept in a woods or in an open field, and went
hungry. Sometimes he was covered with snow when he
awoke in the morning.

Days passed, and the winter grew fierce. Sometimes it was so cold that Gawain's metal armor seemed to burn like fire. He rode through howling blizzards, when he could see nothing but swirling snow all around him. He rode through storms of sleet that left his armor coated with ice.

The land through which he rode grew ever wilder. He passed distant mountains over which hung the smoke of dragons' fiery breath. He saw giants striding in the distance. Twice as tall as a man, they wore garments made of animal skins and carried clubs made of tree trunks. And, once, Gawain was pursued by a band of goblins—short, fat, shaggy, manlike creatures with hideous faces.

Gawain lost track of the days. He knew it must be
nearly Christmas by now. At Camelot, his friends would
be gathered to feast with King Arthur. Gawain wished
he could be with them. He wished he could turn back.
But he had given his word to the Green Knight. He
must go on, even though he was going to his death.

Finally, he felt certain he must be near the Green
Chapel. He rode beside an icy stream that wound
beneath a jagged cliff. He came to a cave and peered
inside. The walls of the cave were covered with green
moss. Could this be the Green Chapel?

Gawain dismounted from his horse. "Green Knight,"
he called, "Gawain is here."

"I bid you welcome, Gawain," said a voice behind
him.

Gawain turned. The Green Knight stood there,
looking at him with eyes that gleamed like emeralds. He
held a great war ax.

"You timed your journey well, Gawain," the Green
Knight said. "It is New Year's Day. Kneel down now
and receive my blow as I received yours twelve months
ago at Camelot!"

Silently, Gawain knelt and bent his head. The Green
Knight stepped close to him. Gawain knew he was
raising the ax. In a moment it would come crashing
down to end his life! In spite of himself, Gawain
flinched and jerked his head to one side.

"What is this?" said the Green Knight. "Do you
flinch without even feeling the blow? I did not flinch
when you swung your sword at me!"

Gawain felt ashamed. He bent his head again, and
stretched his neck. "Strike your blow," he said. "I will
not flinch again."

He heard the swish of the ax as it sliced through the air. But instead of a shattering blow that ended his life, he felt only a tap on his shoulder!

"Rise, Sir Gawain," said the Green Knight. "You have passed the test. You are not to die!"

Gawain rose to his feet and stared in surprise. The Green Knight was gone. In his place was an ordinary man, clad in plain armor.

"I am called Bercilak de Hautdesert," said the man. "I was put under a spell of enchantment by the sorceress, Morgan le Fay, in order to make this test. We wished to find out if the Knights of the Round Table are truly as brave and honorable as they are said to be."

He put his hand on Gawain's shoulder. "You have proved that they are, Gawain. You suffered hunger and hardship to keep your pledge—even though you thought keeping your pledge meant your death. No man could be more brave or more honorable!"

Soon, Sir Gawain was riding back toward Camelot. His heart was filled with joy that he was still alive—and filled with pride that he had kept his pledge!

The Evil
Old Witch

This South American Indian tale comes from the
part of South America where the nations of
Argentina, Brazil, and Uruguay come together. It is
probably a few hundred years old. It is the story of a
man who finds that simply being brave isn't
enough—he needs help and luck as well. But, as the
story shows, if a person *is* brave—and keeps on
trying no matter what—help and luck may be there
when they're needed!

The Evil Old Witch

here was once an ancient and evil witch who lived in a great green forest. She was hundreds of years old, but she was tremendously strong and could run faster than any creature in the forest. Her teeth were of iron, she had a tremendous appetite, and she was always hungry. She often raided nearby villages, carrying off dozens of chickens, pigs, goats, and even a cow or two. No one ever tried to stop her. They were much too afraid of her strength and her powerful magic.

In fact, most of the people in the villages near the forest had become used to giving up at least half their animals each year. In each village there was a special yard in which the animals were kept so that the witch could easily find them whenever she came. By making things easy for her, the villagers hoped to keep her satisfied so that she wouldn't take even more animals or do harm to any people.

One year, a baby boy was born in one of the villages. He grew up to become a brave and sturdy young man. And when the time came for this young man to take

some of his animals to the yard so that the witch might
have them, he refused to do so.

"I saw these animals born," said he. "I have cared for
them since they were babies. I have grown to love them.
Why should I give them up to fatten that evil old
creature? She preys upon us like a vampire bat that
drinks the blood of a helpless young calf! We should
fight her!"

"Take care," cried the other villagers. "The witch will
hear of what you have said. She will come and punish
you!"

"I won't wait for her to come to me," said the young
man. "I shall go into the forest and find her. I shall
make her leave us alone if I have to take her life to do
it!"

Then the villagers gave him the name of Brave Heart.
They watched, respectfully, as he took his spear and
started toward the forest.

Brave Heart walked all that day and all the next. He came to a broad clearing in the forest, in the middle of which was a large pond. Tired and hungry, Brave Heart lay down and went to sleep beneath a tree that stood at the water's edge. During the night he had dreadful dreams about horrible things coming up out of the ground and trying to capture him. He awoke, climbed up into the tree, and slept there the rest of the night.

In the morning he was awakened by the sound of someone singing. It wasn't at all a pretty sound. The voice was cracked and squawky, and the words were dreadful. They went something like this:

> Things in the water,
> You belong to me.
> Your lives are now over,
> You're no longer free.
>
> Things in the water,
> Come here to me.
> I'll kill you and eat you,
> As quick as can be!

Peering out from among the leaves, Brave Heart saw that the singer was none other than the dreadful old witch! She had cast a fishnet into the pond, and her

song was a magical spell that was making fish, frogs,
ducks, and other creatures swim straight into the net.
She had a huge pile of dead creatures lying on the
ground at the edge of the pond.

Unfortunately, Brave Heart had left his spear on the
ground beneath the tree. He was also feeling rather
weak because he hadn't eaten anything the day before.
He decided it would be best for him to stay hidden until
he was better able to deal with the witch.

But the witch happened to look up, and she saw him.
She smiled. It was meant to look like a friendly smile,
but it made Brave Heart think of a grinning alligator.

"You look hungry, young man," said the witch. "I
have lots of good things to eat. Why don't you come
join me for breakfast?"

"Oh, I'm fine right here where I am," said Brave Heart.

The witch saw that she couldn't trick him into coming down, so she used another magic spell. She began plucking blades of grass and piling them together until she had a large pile. Upon this pile of grass she sprinkled a magic powder from a bag she carried. As she sprinkled the powder, she chanted her spell.

"To the tree, now
Creep and crawl.
Up the trunk go,
One and all.

To the branch
Where the man does cling,
And to him
Pain and torture bring!

Pinch him, bite him,
One and all,
Until he must
In the water fall!"

As she finished, each blade of grass changed into a large brown ant. At once the hundreds of ants went straight to Brave Heart's tree. They crawled up the trunk and out onto the limb on which he lay. They swarmed all over him, fiercely pinching and biting! It was more than Brave Heart could stand. He let go of the branch and fell headfirst into the pond.

As soon as he touched the water, Brave Heart tried to swim away. But it was no use. He could hear the witch's voice saying her spell—"Things in the water, come here to me"—and he was helpless. He suddenly

found himself tangled in the witch's fishnet along with a lot of fish, frogs, and other pond creatures. They were all dragged up onto the bank together.

Brave Heart tried to fight, but the witch's tremendous strength was too much for him. She simply stuffed him into a large bag along with many other creatures. Then she tossed the bag onto her shoulder and went dashing through the forest to her home, with Brave Heart bouncing and jouncing in the darkness.

When the witch reached home, she hauled Brave Heart out of the bag and flung him into a tiny, dark

room. There he sat, wondering what was to become of him. He thought how foolish he was to believe he could destroy the old witch.

After a long, long time, the door to the little room opened. Light came streaming in. Brave Heart saw a beautiful young woman standing in the doorway.

"Who are you?" he asked.

"I am the witch's slave," the girl answered. "But, now that she has you, you will become her slave and I will be killed and eaten. That is the witch's way. She keeps one slave for a while, until she finds a new one. Then she eats the old one."

"How terrible!" exclaimed Brave Heart. "I cannot bear to think of you being eaten by that evil hag. We must try to escape." He groaned. "Oh, I suppose it's no use. The old witch can run as fast as the wind. She'd catch us before we even got out of the forest."

"There may be a way," said the girl. "The witch has a magic stone that enables her to fly. She seldom uses it, because she can run as fast as the stone can fly. Besides, it only works while the sun is up. I know where she keeps it, but I never dared try to use it for fear the witch would just catch me and kill me. But now I have nothing to lose. At this moment the witch is away gathering firewood. If you are willing to try, I will get the stone. If we can get far enough away before the witch finds out, she may not be able to catch us."

"We must try," said Brave Heart.

The girl hurried off. She was soon back, carrying a large green stone and a bag full of yellow powder. "The witch uses this magic powder to change one kind of thing into another," she told Brave Heart. "It may be useful to us."

Just then, they heard the voice of the witch, right outside the house!

"I have the firewood to roast you with, dear," she called out to the girl. "The boy will be my new slave, so I don't need you any more. I'm going to cook you with salt and chili peppers."

"Quick," said Brave Heart. "We must leave before she comes into the house."

He took the bag of powder in one hand, and the girl's hand in the other. She spoke the word of magic that made the stone fly. At once it lifted the two of them

into the air and carried them right through the only open window in the witch's house.

But the window was right beside the front door, and there stood the witch, just about to open the door. When she saw Brave Heart and the girl fly out of the house, she was astounded. For a moment she just stood and stared. Then she dropped the huge load of firewood she was carrying and began to run after them.

The stone carried Brave Heart and the girl swiftly

over the treetops. But the witch was always right
beneath them, running as fast as the stone could fly,
and glaring up at them with angry red eyes. It was clear
to Brave Heart that he and the girl couldn't fly any
faster than the wicked old creature could run.

To make matters worse, it was very late in the
afternoon. The sun would soon set—and when it went
down, the stone would lose all its magic power. Then
the old witch would have them!

Brave Heart thought of the magic powder he was
carrying. He shook some of it out of the bag. It drifted
down to the ground, falling upon the leaves of a bush.
At once the leaves became rabbits, which went
bounding away in all directions. This was too much for
the always-hungry old witch—she just had to stop and
catch a few rabbits to eat!

So Brave Heart and the girl gained a little distance.
But the sun was red and low in the sky, and the power
of the stone was beginning to fail. Brave Heart and the
girl were dropping closer and closer to the ground, and
were moving more slowly. The witch soon caught up to
them again.

"Soon we will be so low that she will be able to catch
hold of us," said the girl, tearfully. "We are doomed."

But Brave Heart saw that they were heading straight

toward the pond where he had been captured by the
witch. "We can get away from her by crossing the
water," he exclaimed. "She will have to swim across."

"It does not matter," the girl told him. "She can swim
as fast as she can run!"

In desperation, Brave Heart flung down a handful of
the magic powder. It drifted onto some large rocks at
the edge of the pond, and the rocks turned into big
turtles. Once again the hungry witch couldn't resist the
sight of so much food. She grabbed up an armful of the
turtles and swallowed them whole, one after another,
shells and all!

Brave Heart and the girl drifted slowly over the pond. By the time they reached the other side, their toes were nearly touching the water. Right at the edge of the pond, the stone's power gave out. The girl and Brave Heart found themselves standing on the ground.

They turned to look back at the pond. The witch was swimming toward them. The setting sun had turned the water red, and it looked as if the witch were swimming through blood! She angrily gnashed her teeth at the two young people.

Brave Heart and the girl knew the witch would soon be upon them. Then she would tear them to pieces with her clawlike fingernails. They put their arms around one another, each trying to comfort the other.

But—something was happening! The witch was moving more slowly. She seemed to be sinking!

"The turtles," cried Brave Heart. "She ate all those big, heavy turtles and now they are weighing her down!"

It was true. The witch was splashing furiously, but hardly moving. Shrieking with fury, she sank lower and lower in the water. At last, they could see only her red eyes, glaring at them. Then, she disappeared beneath the water and was gone forever.

Brave Heart and the girl hugged each other as hard as they could, and danced for joy. Next morning, using the magic stone, they flew back to Brave Heart's village. There they were married.

"You have done what you set out to do, Brave Heart," said the villagers. "You have destroyed the evil old witch so that she will never bother us again."

But Brave Heart shook his head. "I did not do anything," he said. "It was really all my brave wife's doing—with the help of some heavy turtles!"

The City Without a King

This tale comes from Burma, a nation that lies between India and China. The people of Burma are much like the people of China. The hero of the story is the sort of person they respect—wise and polite, as well as brave and strong.

The City Without a King

In olden times in the land of Burma there was a young man by the name of Pauk Kyaing. His parents wanted him to become a wise and honored scholar, and so they sent him to the great university, where he could study under learned teachers.

However, it turned out that Pauk Kyaing was not a good student. He fell asleep while his teachers explained things. He did not care to study the books filled with ancient wisdom. And he had no wise or clever ideas of his own.

The one thing that Pauk Kyaing could do well was to use a sword. When he practiced swordfighting with other students he always beat them easily. Not only was he a skillful swordsman, he was also very strong—he could chop a log of teakwood in two with a single blow of his sword!

One day the head of the university asked Pauk Kyaing to come and talk with him. "You will never be a scholar, my son," said he, sadly. "You are good only at using a sword, so perhaps you should become a soldier.

But to stay on here at the school would be a waste of time. It would be best if you left."

"I suppose so, honored teacher," said the young man. He was glad that he would no longer have to try to become a scholar, but he was sorry that he had not been able to do what his parents wanted.

"Before you go, please let me give you three valuable pieces of wisdom," said the old teacher. "They will truly help you in your life. Listen carefully, now, and try to remember them.

"You can have a happy ending to a journey only after you have traveled far.

"You can learn that which is truly worth knowing only by asking many questions.

"You can have a long life only if you stay awake more than you sleep."

"I shall truly remember these three things, honored teacher," said Pauk Kyaing, earnestly. "I thank you."

Carrying his few belongings in a bag, the young man set out to return home. He had traveled for most of a day when he came to a branch in the road. Pauk Kyaing knew that if he took the road that went to the left he would soon be home. But the other road would take him far out of his way. If he took it, he might not get home for months.

He thought of the first of the three wise sayings his teacher had asked him to remember: "You can have a happy ending to a journey only after you have traveled far."

Pauk Kyaing had great respect for his teacher. "Very well," he said to himself, "I shall travel far before I go home." He took the road that went to the right.

He walked for several days without meeting a single person. Then one morning he came to the banks of the Irrawaddy River. On the other side of the river was a splendid city, over which towered a magnificent palace.

Pauk Kyaing wondered what city this might be, and who its ruler was. He then remembered the second of the three things his teacher had told him: "You can learn that which is truly worth knowing only by asking many questions." Seeing an old man coming toward him from the direction of the city, Pauk Kyaing decided to question him.

"Pardon me, Old and Honorable Sir," said he, bowing. "Can you tell me the name of that city?"

"Yes, indeed," said the old man. "It is the city of Tagaung."

"Who is the king of Tagaung?" asked Pauk Kyaing. He thought he might go and see if the king would hire him as a soldier.

"Alas, there is no king," said the old one. "A curse lies upon Tagaung! Two years ago there was a young prince who was to become king. But the day before he was to be crowned, and married to the beautiful princess who would be his queen, he was dreadfully and mysteriously slain! He was found in the king's bedroom—torn to pieces as if he had been attacked by some huge, terrible beast!"

"Dreadful!" exclaimed Pauk Kyaing.

"The people of Tagaung grieved, but they knew they must have a king," the old man went on. "So they sent word to a young prince in a distant land, offering to make him king and let him marry the princess. He accepted joyfully and came to Tagaung. But, he, too, was found in the king's bedroom next morning—torn to bits!"

"Strange and frightening," murmured Pauk Kyaing.

"After that, the people of Tagaung offered to let any man be king who could stay alive during a night in the king's bedroom," said the man. "Many men tried, at first, but they were all slain the same way. Now, no one else dares try." He shook his head, sadly. "The throne is still empty, and the princess still waits to become a queen."

Pauk Kyaing thought very hard for a few moments. It seemed to him that so far the two wise sayings he had followed had helped him. One had led him to take the road to this city. The other had prompted him to ask the questions that revealed that any man could become king of the city. Now he wondered if the third saying

might hold the answer to *how* a man could become
king. "You can have a long life only if you stay awake
more than you sleep," was the saying. Perhaps that
meant a man could stay alive during a night in the
royal bedroom if he simply stayed awake.

"How does a man let the people of Tagaung know he
is willing to try to become their king?" Pauk Kyaing
asked the old man.

"It is quite easy," the man told him. "Next to the
palace gate there hangs a gong. A man simply strikes
the gong. Servants will then come and lead him to the
king's bedroom." Suddenly, a startled look came upon

the old man's face. "Surely you are not going to try?"
he cried. "Do not be foolish! You are too young to die
in such a dreadful way!"

"I thank you for your kind warning, Old and
Honorable Sir," said Pauk Kyaing, bowing. "But I feel
that I must try."

And so Pauk Kyaing marched down the road to the
edge of the river. There, he hired a boat to take him
across the river to the city. Reaching the palace gate, he
saw that a large bronze gong hung next to it, as the old
man had said. He struck the gong hard with his fist. It
made a long, loud, shimmering sound.

Shortly, two servants came to the gate and beckoned
to Pauk Kyaing. Without a word they led him into the
palace, down a long corridor, and into a large room.
Then they bowed and left, closing the door behind them.

Pauk Kyaing looked around. The room was the king's bedroom. It was the most beautiful room he had ever seen. The walls were of polished wood, carved with beautiful designs. In the center of the room was a huge pillar made from a giant tree trunk. It was so thick that two men could not stretch out their arms and join hands around it. This great pillar had been smoothed and polished until it gleamed like gold.

At the base of this huge pillar was the royal bed, with pillows covered in silk and sheets of satin. It looked most comfortable to Pauk Kyaing, who was quite tired. He would dearly love to sleep in such a fine bed.

However, Pauk Kyaing had made up his mind not to sleep a wink while he was in this room. He was sure that the third wise saying meant that this was not the time to go to sleep, that he had a better chance of staying alive if he stayed awake.

He took two of the silken pillows and wrapped them in a satin sheet. He placed them on the bed and covered them with another sheet. Now it looked as if someone were lying in the bed. Then Pauk Kyaing went to a corner of the room and sat down with his back against the wall. Holding his sword in his lap, he waited—for whatever was going to happen.

The room began to grow dark as night fell outside. Pauk Kyaing sat clutching his sword and waiting. Once or twice he felt himself beginning to doze. At once he shook his head to awaken himself. He thought again of the wise saying: "You can have a long life only if you stay awake more than you sleep."

Shortly after midnight, Pauk Kyaing became aware that the room was growing lighter. The light was coming from the huge tree trunk pillar. The trunk

seemed to be splitting open. A golden light was
streaming out of the opening.

Something else was coming out of the opening as well.
A long, scaly snout poked out. Red eyes glowed and
sharp teeth gleamed. Next came a long, snaky neck
followed by a big, scaly body. It was a dragon spirit that
lived in the tree trunk! This must be the creature that
had slain all the young men!

In an instant, the dragon pounced upon the bed. Its
teeth sank into the pillows Pauk Kyaing had placed
there. Before the creature realized it had been tricked,
Pauk Kyaing sprang forward. With all his mighty

strength he struck a blow that sliced the dragon's head
from its body.

When the servants came to the royal bedroom in the
morning, they found Pauk Kyaing alive and sitting on
the body of the dead dragon. And so Pauk Kyaing
became king of Tagaung because he had been strong
and brave enough to kill the dragon—and wise enough
to pay attention to his teacher's three wise sayings.

The Many-Headed Monster

This story, which is thousands of years old, comes
from the land of Hellas, which we now call Greece.
It is one of many stories about a great hero in Greek
mythology. His Greek name is Heracles, but he is
usually called Hercules, the name used by the
Romans.

Hercules, like many Greek heroes, was the son of a
god. His mother was Alcmene, a mortal, and his
father was Zeus, king of the gods. In all the stories
told about him, Hercules is tremendously strong and
absolutely fearless. He is the kind of hero that the
people of ancient Greece most admired. However, he
isn't a "perfect" person. He sometimes does foolish
and even cruel things. Perhaps the people who made
up the stories about him wanted to show that even
great heroes have faults.

The Many-Headed Monster

ear the city of Lerna there lay a great, deep
swamp. At the edge of the swamp stood a small forest.
No farmhouse or shepherd's hut was near this place, for
no man, woman, or child could live there. Over swamp
and forest there hung a pale, gray mist that reeked with
a foul and poisonous odor. Death came to any person
who breathed that mist for too long a time!

No ordinary mist was this—it was the breath of a
monster! The swamp and forest were the abode of a
horrible creature known as the Hydra. Its body was the
body of a huge dog, and from its neck grew nine
snakelike heads. Each head breathed out the deadly,
poisonous fumes that formed the mist.

Every year, the mist crept outward a little farther and
covered a bit more of the land. In Lerna, the people
worried and wondered, knowing there would be a day
when the mist would finally creep into their city. But
there seemed nothing they could do. How could so
fearsome a monster as the Hydra be destroyed?

Then, one day, a chariot drawn by handsome white

horses rumbled up the narrow road that passed by the swamp. A young man guided the chariot with skillful tugs on the horses' reins. Beside him stood another man, as tall as a giant and as sturdy as a young bull. When the chariot reached the edge of the gray mist that curled over the swamp, the driver pulled on the reins, tugging the horses to a stop. The man beside him leaped to the ground.

Around his head and shoulders, this young giant wore the golden-brown skin of a huge lion. In his hand he held a thick wooden club cut from the stout limb of a wild olive tree. He had dark, fierce eyes, and his bulging muscles looked as if they were cast from bronze metal. None other than Hercules was he, the most famed hero throughout the length and breadth of the land of Hellas.

Even when he was but a babe, only ten months old, Hercules had shown the strength and courage of a hero. One night, as he lay asleep, two deadly serpents

slithered into his crib, their sharp fangs dripping with
poison. But the baby Hercules awoke and saw them.
Seizing a serpent in each hand, he strangled the
creatures to death before they could harm him!

Now that Hercules was a grown man, he used his
strength, skill, courage, and wisdom to help all those in
danger and trouble. It was to help the people of Lerna
that he had come to the misty swamp. He had come to
do battle with the Hydra and destroy it! Peering
through the drifting mist, he tried to catch sight of the
hideous beast. But he saw nothing.

Then the driver of the chariot, whose name was
Iolaus, spoke. "There it is, Hercules, beneath the
branches of that sycamore tree."

The hero turned his eyes to where Iolaus pointed.
Now, he, too, saw the dreaded Hydra, lying asleep

beneath the tree. But between Hercules and the
monster lay many pools of water and patches of muddy,
marshy ground.

Said Hercules, "The ground between us is too wet
and uneven to give good footing for a fight. I must
make the beast come forth to me—here, where the
ground is firm. I shall anger it with fiery arrows."

Then Hercules and Iolaus gathered brush and
branches and kindled a fire. Hercules held arrows in the
flame until they began to blaze. Then he loosed them at
the Hydra. A rain of fiery arrows sped through the air.

The Hydra awoke in a dreadful rage. Each of its nine
heads hissing with anger, it leaped toward the hero.

"Move back, good Iolaus," counseled Hercules.
Holding his stout wooden club, the mighty hero awaited
his enemy. Hercules had many fine swords, spears, and
other weapons, but the club served him best of all. He
also had fine armor, a helmet, and a shield, but he
preferred to wear the tough skin of the lion that he
himself had slain, for it protected him well.

As the monster came rushing at him, Hercules drew in a deep breath. Well did he know that if he breathed the Hydra's poisonous breath, which could kill most people, he might grow weak and giddy. Holding his breath, he stepped forward and seized the beast by one of its necks. With a mighty blow, he crushed one of the snaky heads.

But the Hydra possessed strange powers! If one of its heads was destroyed, another grew in its place! Each time the mighty Hercules swung his club and smashed one of the Hydra's heads, another appeared! Putting aside his club, Hercules drew his sword. Now he began to lop off the Hydra's heads, but to no avail. As fast as he cut off one head, a new one grew in its place.

Iolaus saw that things were not going well. He knew Hercules could not hold his breath much longer. Snatching up a burning branch from the fire, Iolaus sped to Hercules' side. Then, each time the hero cut off one of the Hydra's heads, Iolaus seared the stump of the neck with his torch so that a new head could not grow. In this way, eight of the monster's heads were destroyed forever.

Then, with one last blow, Hercules cut off the ninth head. But the ninth head of the Hydra could not be destroyed, for, lo, it was immortal! Still alive, the head continued to hiss and breathe out poison. But the mighty Hercules lifted up a huge boulder. Placing the boulder over the Hydra's undying head, he buried it for all time.

Thus was the dreadful Hydra vanquished by the mighty hero of Hellas. With time, the poisonous mist grew thinner and at last dissolved away. The city of Lerna was saved and greatly did its people rejoice.

The Quest
for the Sampo

More than one hundred years ago in Finland, a
country doctor by the name of Elias Lonnröot went
about seeking centuries-old songs, poems, and
chants. He wrote down everything he heard, so that
it would never be lost. He formed all these ancient
legends into a poem called the *Kalevala,* meaning
"Land of Heroes." This was the name the Finnish
people called their country long, long ago when these
tales were first told.

The *Kalevala* is now the national epic, or
adventure-poem, of Finland. The story of the quest
for the Sampo is a portion of the *Kalevala.*

257

The Quest for the Sampo

n the Land of Heroes there dwelt two
brothers. One was the old and crafty singer and
magician, Vainamoinen. The other was Ilmarinen the
smith, a skilled maker of metal tools and weapons.

To the far north, to the land of Pohjola, Ilmarinen
had gone. There he toiled hard for the queen, Louhi, to
make a marvelous magic mill, the Sampo, that would
grind out corn, salt, and golden coins. With the Sampo,
Pohjola would be a land of plenty for all eternity.

High up in the mountains of Pohjola, Ilmarinen built
a huge forge and a fierce fire. Into the forge he threw
the magical ingredients—the point of a swan's feather, a
drop of cow's milk, a single grain of barley, and a curl of
lamb's wool. Then Ilmarinen sang words of magic until
the ingredients flowed together and formed a lump of
magic metal.

Each day, with great, ringing blows of his hammer,
Ilmarinen beat the hot metal into shape. On the first
day, it formed the shape of a golden bow. On the second
day, he beat the bow into the shape of a bronze boat.

On the third day, he beat the boat into a copper cow with golden horns. The fourth day, the cow became a golden plow with a silver handle. And on the fifth day, Ilmarinen saw that he had turned the plow into the Sampo.

For all his work, Ilmarinen was to have had Louhi's daughter as his wife. However, a wicked magician, Kullervo, also wanted the girl. Rather than let Ilmarinen have her, Kullervo turned the girl's herd of cows into wolves and bears—and they ate her! So, although Louhi had the Sampo, Ilmarinen still had no wife. He returned to the Land of Heroes glum and grumbling.

"It is not fair," he exclaimed to his brother, Vainamoinen. "The Sampo sits in Pohjola to this day,

grinding out corn, and salt, and golden coins for Louhi and her people. But I have no wife to keep me company and cook my meat!"

"Indeed, it is not fair," old Vainamoinen agreed. "It seems to me that the Sampo more truly belongs here in the Land of Heroes than in wild and far-off Pohjola. Let us get it and bring it back here!"

"Ah, that we could not do, my brother," said Ilmarinen, shaking his head. "It is kept deep in a cave within a copper mountain, held fast by nine magic locks. And it is far too big for just two men to carry, even though they be heroes such as we."

"Let us go anyway," urged the lively Vainamoinen, with a grin. "We shall find a ship big enough to carry the Sampo for us."

They armed themselves and rode toward the sea. As they rode along the shore, they came to an old ship that had been pulled up onto the sand and left there. The ship was sobbing quietly to itself.

"Ship, why do you weep?" asked Vainamoinen, bringing his horse to a stop.

"Ah, I weep because here I sit alone and forgotten," said the ship. "Snakes crawl beneath my keel and birds build nests in my masts. But I was made for the sea!"

"Could you still carry people?" Vainamoinen asked.

"I could carry a thousand strong oarsmen," boasted the ship.

"Well, brother, here is the ship that will take us to Pohjola and carry the Sampo back for us," said old Vainamoinen. He began to sing words of magic. A hundred sturdy young men with oars appeared along one side of the boat. A hundred young women with oars appeared along the other side. A large group of old people appeared in the middle.

"Let us be off to Pohjola," Vainamoinen cried. Ilmarinen shoved the ship into the sea. The young men and girls began to row, while the old people chanted to help them keep time. The ship slid happily through the bright blue water.

After some time, the ship passed near a bit of land on which stood some little houses. A man came running out of one of the houses and waved at the ship. He was none other than the young hero, Lemminkainen, who was also a skilled magician.

"Hail, Vainamoinen and Ilmarinen," he called. "Where are you bound?"

"We sail to the land of Pohjola, to seize the Sampo and bring it back to the Land of Heroes," answered Vainamoinen.

"Then take me with you," urged Lemminkainen. "For you may have to fight, and I am a mighty fighter, as you know."

"Come aboard," said the wise Vainamoinen. And so Lemminkainen made a great running leap and sailed over the water to land in the ship.

The ship sailed on, always keeping near the coast. The young men and women rowed steadily. The old men chanted. While Vainamoinen steered, he asked Ahto, the god of the sea, for his aid. And Lemminkainen sang spells to protect the ship from such evil water spirits as the wicked Vetehinen and the monster Iku-Turso.

Suddenly, with a great thump, the ship struck something and stopped motionless in the water. Lemminkainen peered over the side.

"We have run into a giant fish," he cried.

"So we have," said Vainamoinen. Leaning out over the side of the ship he struck a mighty blow with his sword and cut the huge fish in two. Using his sword as a fork, he lifted the two halves out of the water and dropped them onto the deck. "Here's a fine supper for all of us," he cried. "Let's go ashore and cook it."

They steered the ship toward the shore, built a fire on the beach, and cooked the fish. Everyone enjoyed the fine supper. When all were finished, there was nothing left except the giant pike's big bones, gleaming in the pale moonlight.

"I wonder what might be done with these?" said wise Vainamoinen, staring at the bones and scratching his beard in thought.

"Nothing," Ilmarinen told him. "What can you do with a lot of old fishbones?"

But the longer clever old Vainamoinen looked at the bones, the more he saw they were just the right shape for the frame of a kantele, a five-stringed harplike instrument. So, using the giant pike's jawbones, and some of the girls' hair for strings, he made a kantele. Sitting down on the beach, he began to play and sing.

Beautiful beyond compare were the songs of Vainamoinen, for the wise old sorcerer knew well the secret magic of music. As he played and sang, the animals came creeping out of the woods to listen. The eagles left their nests on the high mountainsides and came gliding overhead to hear. The creatures of the sea came swimming in toward the shore.

Tears fell from the eyes of every man and woman who heard Vainamoinen's voice, and the very spirits of the wind, the water, and the woods paused to listen. All

through the night Vainamoinen played, and all through
the next day and the next night. Then, with a sigh, he
tucked the kantele under his arm. "Let us be on our
way," he said.

The ship sped through the sea until, at last, the three
heroes saw the dark land of Pohjola looming in the
distance. They steered for the shore and pulled the ship
up onto the beach. Then they set out for the house of
Queen Louhi. Fearlessly, they strode into her guesthall.

Louhi looked at them with eyes as black as a
midnight sky. "Why are you here, men of Kalevala?"
she asked in an icy voice.

"We have come to let you share your Sampo with us," answered the saucy Vainamoinen, with a smile.

"Why should I do that?" asked the queen, and lifted her hand in a signal. At once, the three heroes were surrounded by a ring of spears in the hands of many grim warriors.

But Vainamoinen had his kantele under his arm. Smiling, he began to play and sing. Soft and drowsy was the music, filled with a spell of sleep. The eyes of Louhi and her warriors began to close. Soon, they all sank to the floor in slumber.

"Now, let us get the Sampo and be gone," whispered the sly Vainamoinen.

To the copper mountain they hurried, and entered the cave where the Sampo lay hidden. There it was, gleaming and glowing in the darkness, held in place by nine sturdy, magical locks. But these Ilmarinen opened, one after another, with spells, strength, and skill. Then Lemminkainen put his arms around the Sampo. With a mighty heave, he tore it loose from the rocky floor.

Helped by the other two heroes, Lemminkainen carried the Sampo down to where their ship lay upon the shore. They placed the gleaming Sampo on the deck and pushed the ship into the water. The young men and girls began to row, and the ship shot out onto the blue sea.

"Ho, what a great, wonderful, and magnificent deed have we three heroes done!" exclaimed the lively Lemminkainen, dancing upon the deck. "Play a gay tune on your kantele, Vainamoinen, and let us celebrate!"

"We are not yet out of danger," warned the wise Vainamoinen. "It will be best to wait until we have the Sampo safely home in the Land of Heroes before we celebrate."

But the rash Lemminkainen only laughed at the wise Vainamoinen's words of caution. Then he began to sing at the top of his lungs. So loud was the noise he made that it carried over the water, the plain, and the woods, and woke Queen Louhi from her magical slumber.

She gazed at her sleeping warriors. "I fear those three men from Kalevala have done us great harm," said she, grimly. Hurrying to the copper mountain, she saw that the Sampo was gone. In dreadful rage, she stood upon the mountainside and called down curses upon Vainamoinen, Ilmarinen, and Lemminkainen!

"Spirits of Darkness, keep them from escaping," she shrieked. "Uutar, Spirit of Fogs, wrap them in mist so they cannot find their way! Iku-Turso, Spirit of the Sea, pull them down into the depths! Ukko, Lord of the Sky, send a storm to smash their ship and cast them into the sea!"

A powerful witch was Louhi, and the spirits she had called upon obeyed her. A thick, white fog came creeping over the sea, sent by Uutar, the Spirit of Fogs. It closed around the heroes' ship so that they could not see.

"This is Louhi's doing," muttered Vainamoinen. "She seeks to keep us from reaching the Land of Heroes."

For three days the ship drifted in the fog. Many spells did Vainamoinen try in an effort to drive the fog away. At last, late on the third day, he succeeded. The fog suddenly vanished. The heroes found that the ship was far from land, and headed in the wrong direction!

But now they could see which way to steer, so the ship was turned around and the young men and women began rowing again. Everyone's spirits rose as the ship sped toward the Land of Heroes.

However, wise Vainamoinen felt sure that Louhi would try something else to keep them from getting safely home. "I will keep watch tonight, while the others sleep," said he to himself.

It was well, indeed, that he did. For in the middle of the night, as moonlight shimmered upon the black water, a huge and horrible monster rose up from the sea! It was Iku-Turso, Spirit of the Sea. Placing his slimy claws upon the ship, the great beast tried to pull it under the waves. But forward sprang the watchful Vainamoinen, with upraised sword.

Well did Iku-Turso know of Vainamoinen's power, and greatly did he fear him. "Hold, wise Vainamoinen," he cried in a voice that rumbled like thunder. "Spare me, and I pledge to nevermore do harm to you or any mortal man!"

"Depart then," ordered Vainamoinen, and the monster sank back into the sea.

But now that both Uutar, Spirit of the Fogs, and Iku-Turso, Spirit of the Sea, had failed, the third of Louhi's curses struck the heroes. With a fearsome shriek, a mighty wind raced over the sea, sent by Ukko, Lord of the Sky. The wind scooped up huge waves and sent them smashing into the heroes' ship. The ship pitched and tossed and shuddered in the wild sea!

Then did Vainamoinen begin singing spells to ward off the storm's fury, while Lemminkainen made magic to repair the damage done by the waves. In time, the storm died away, and the ship was still safely afloat. And in the distance could be seen the shoreline of the Land of Heroes.

But the curses of Louhi had done their work by delaying the heroes. Now, as Lemminkainen looked out over the sea, he beheld, speeding toward them, a huge, black ship. It was rowed by a hundred men, with a thousand grim warriors crowded on the deck. At the front of the ship, her eyes blazing with rage and hate, was Queen Louhi!

"A warship of Pohjola," cried Lemminkainen. "It will overtake us before we can reach shore!"

Vainamoinen saw that they would have no chance in a battle with so many warriors of Pohjola. He searched his mind for some spell to use against them. Then he pulled forth his tinderbox, which held a piece of flint

stone and a lump of steel. When struck together, these
made a spark to start a fire. Hurling the piece of flint
into the sea, Vainamoinen sang out a spell.

"Flint, become a jagged reef,
And bring Queen Louhi's ship to grief!"

At once the piece of flint became a huge, sharp-edged
rock, jutting up out of the water in the path of Louhi's
ship. Before the oarsmen of Pohjola could turn the ship,
it smashed headlong into the reef and broke apart. It
began to sink.

But Louhi shrieked out a spell of her own. Her body
swelled and she became a giant. Seizing some of the

warriors' swords, she fixed them to her fingers, making
long, terrible claws. Grasping the broken sides of the
ship, she turned them into huge, wooden wings. Like a
great, terrible bird, she flew at the ship of the three heroes.

Down she swooped, and perched upon the ship's rail.
The ship leaned far over from her great weight. But the
lively Lemminkainen leaped forward. With his sword, he
cut away all the sword-tipped fingers of her right hand.
At his side, the lusty Vainamoinen swung his sword and
cut off all but one of the fingers of her left hand.

Dreadful to hear was Louhi's shriek of rage and despair as she began to slip into the sea. With her one finger, she reached out and seized the Sampo lying on the deck. Clutching the Sampo, she fell into the water. As the Sampo struck the water, it broke apart. Louhi was left with only one tiny piece. Her dark eyes glared at Vainamoinen. "I shall have my revenge," she screamed in fury. Then she turned and began to swim toward the north, back to frozen and foggy Pohjola.

Sadly did old Vainamoinen gaze down into the water where the Sampo had fallen. Gone forever, it seemed, was the world's greatest treasure. But then his eyes lit up with joy. He saw that pieces of the Sampo were floating to the surface and were drifting in toward the shore of the Land of Heroes!

Then Vainamoinen set the young men and women rowing for shore. He leaped onto the land and hurried along the beach, picking up pieces of the Sampo. Each piece was still full of magic, and all of them together were nearly as powerful as the whole Sampo had been! Thus the magic of the Sampo came to the Land of

Heroes, where it truly belonged. Then did peace, happiness, and wealth fill all that land.

In dark and foggy Pohjola, Louhi ground her teeth in anger when she heard how the pieces of the Sampo were bringing good luck, good crops, and wealth to the Land of Heroes. For many long days she brooded on how to punish Vainamoinen and his people. Finally, she decided. In the dark of night she performed foul magic, and sent forth nine evil demons and monsters to spread death and disease throughout the Land of Heroes.

Soon the wailing of sick and miserable people echoed across the land. But wise old Vainamoinen knew what was happening, and knew what to do. With powerful magic, he drove the horrors sent by Louhi up into the mountains and sealed them in a cave. Then with soothing, magical medicines he healed the sick and saddened people of the Land of Heroes, until all were well again.

Hearing of this in frozen Pohjola, Louhi again made

dire magic. She awakened the huge and terrible Bear of
the Frozen Plains from its slumber and sent it snarling
into the Land of Heroes. It smashed its way through
village after village. All fled in fear before it.

But again, dependable Vainamoinen knew what to do.
He had Ilmarinen forge a spear of shining copper, into
which Vainamoinen wove strong spells. Then did the
brave old magician hurry forth to battle the bear! Back
he came, ere long, dragging the bear behind him—dead!
Its skin was made into warm garments, and its flesh
was simmered until it became a tasty feast for all the
people for many leagues around.

Now did Louhi's rage and hatred become as a roaring forest fire. Summoning all the powers of darkness at her disposal, she performed a deed so dreadful that it put the world into danger! For, from where it perched atop a fir tree, she stole the sun! And from where it hung among the branches of a birch, she took the moon! She carried them into the far northern mountains of Pohjola. There she hid them deep in a mountain of iron, behind locked doors bound with chains.

And so, save for the dim twinkle of the stars, all light went out of the world and cold came creeping in. In the Land of Heroes, the crops grew hard and brittle from frost. The cattle froze where they stood. The people huddled in their dark houses, weeping.

Grimly did old Vainamoinen use his magic to find where the sun and moon had been hidden. Then he made his way to his brother's workplace.

"Now you must forge me a dozen sharp axes, brother," said he. "I must have them to chop through the chains that bind the doors in the iron mountain. Forge me a dozen keys to unlock the doors. And forge me a collar of iron to fit around the neck of Louhi!"

Ilmarinen donned his apron of oxhide and heated the fires of his forge. Soon the land was filled with the ringing of his hammer as he beat the hot, soft metal into axes, keys, and a collar. The wind carried the sound through the darkness to distant Pohjola, where Louhi heard it and wondered what it meant. She turned herself into a gray hawk and flew to the Land of Heroes to find out.

She came to where Ilmarinen was working and perched in a tree to watch him. "What are you forging, O Greatest of Smiths?" she asked.

"Axes to chop through chains. Keys to unlock doors. And a collar to fit around the neck of Louhi so that she can be chained to a mountainside forever," answered Ilmarinen.

Then Louhi was filled with fear. She saw that Vainamoinen intended dreadful punishment for what she had done. Swiftly she flew back to frozen Pohjola. Straight to the iron mountain she went. Unchaining the doors and flinging them open, she freed the sun and moon, carried them outside, and put them back in place.

The Land of Heroes grew bright and warm again. Vainamoinen looked up and saw that the sun and moon were once more where they belonged. Picking up his kantele, he began to play and sing. Men, women, and children came rushing forth to dance and listen to the magic of his music. All was well in the Land of Heroes, and never again did Louhi dare make mischief.

The Wicked Enchantment

This is one of many tales about King Arthur and his Knights of the Round Table. It was probably told in parts of Britain more than a thousand years ago.

In most of the King Arthur tales, the hero is a brave knight who risks his life against all kinds of dangers. But this is the tale not of a hero but of a heroine, of a young woman who risks her life to save one of Arthur's knights from a horrible death.

The Wicked Enchantment

mong the knights who served King Arthur
were two brave young warriors by the names of Sir
Caradoc and Sir Cador. They were firm friends, as close
as if they were brothers. In fact, they were to become
brothers-in-law, for Sir Caradoc was to marry Sir
Cador's sister, the beautiful Lady Guimier.

Like all of King Arthur's knights, Cador and Caradoc
believed it their duty to fight against evil and injustice.
They spent much of their time riding throughout the
land, using their strength and bravery to help people.
But in doing this, it happened that Sir Caradoc put
himself in great peril.

He punished a wicked noblewoman who was causing
hardship and suffering to a great many people. The
woman swore to have revenge. She sought out a
powerful magician known as Eliaures the Enchanter,
who agreed to help her against Caradoc.

One day Caradoc was riding through a forest at
sunset. Stopping in a glade beside a stream, he began to
make camp for the night. After taking off his armor, he

pitched his tent and sat dozing before his campfire.
Suddenly a wintery chill came over the glade. The fire
flickered and went out. Caradoc looked up and beheld a
tall man in a hooded robe. The stranger gazed at him
with eyes that seemed to burn a fiery red!

"Who are you?" exclaimed Caradoc.

"I am Eliaures the Enchanter," said the man. "I bring
you the vengeance of the Lady Morgaine."

He stretched forth his hand toward Sir Caradoc.
Clutched in his fist was a small, slim, green serpent.
The snake's yellow eyes glared at the young knight, and
its tongue flickered in its red mouth as it hissed with
hatred. Then there was a sudden flash of light. Caradoc
felt a burning pain in his arm. Looking down, he saw
with horror that the serpent was now coiled around his
arm and its jaws were fastened in his flesh!

Caradoc leaped to his feet and grasped the snake firmly, to pull it off. But he found that no matter how hard he tugged, the horrible creature would not budge. He drew his dagger to slash the snake and kill it. But the sharp blade made not a mark on the creature's scaly skin.

"It is no use, Sir Caradoc," said the magician. "The serpent can never be slain nor removed. It will stay with you, sucking away the blood and flesh of your body until you die. You are doomed!" With that, he vanished.

Caradoc did everything he could to rid himself of the dreadful serpent. He traveled to see wise doctors and visited skilled magicians. But no one could remove the deadly snake from his arm. Each day, Caradoc found himself becoming weaker and weaker. His arm was now thin and shriveled.

Finally, Caradoc decided there was nothing that could be done for him. He would simply grow thinner and

weaker until he died. He was doomed, as Eliaures had told him. Sadly, the young knight rode to the castle that was his home, to die there.

Word of Caradoc's awful plight soon reached King Arthur's court, at Camelot, where Sir Cador and the Lady Guimier were staying. At once, these two set out to go to Caradoc's aid. Guimier felt certain that if she could look after Caradoc and nurse him, her love would keep him alive.

But when Caradoc learned they were coming to his castle, he wept. He was now weak and gaunt, his eyes dark and hollow. And the arm to which the snake was fastened was like the bony arm of a skeleton. Caradoc did not want his beloved Guimier to see him in this terrible condition. That night he left the castle, letting no one see him go, and rode to a distant monastery. He begged the priests to let him stay there until he died.

Thus, when Sir Cador and the Lady Guimier arrived at Caradoc's castle, he was gone and no one knew where. "He has hidden himself from us because he is ashamed to let us see what the wicked enchantment has done to him," sobbed Guimier. "You must search for him, Cador. You must find him before it is too late."

"I vow that I will not rest until I find him," declared Sir Cador.

He set forth at once, seeking some word or sign of his friend. He asked about Caradoc at lonely farmhouses and in crowded villages. He searched through forests and in caves. And, in time, he came to the monastery in which Caradoc lay dying. When the priests saw that Cador was a true friend to Caradoc, they took him to the young knight's room.

"Ah, Caradoc, it grieves me to see you like this," cried

Cador. "Tell me, dear friend, who has done this terrible thing to you?"

"Eliaures the Enchanter," whispered Caradoc in a weak voice.

"I shall seek out this Eliaures and make him end this wicked enchantment," Sir Cador cried, pounding his fist on the table.

"Beware," warned Caradoc. "He is a powerful magician and an evil man! There is no telling what he might do to you."

Sir Cador set out again, this time to search for Eliaures. It was easy to find the magician, for many people knew of him. However, he lived in a castle guarded by dangerous magical creatures and enchantments. It was certain death for anyone to enter Eliaures' castle without the magician's permission.

But Sir Cador drew his sword and strode through the castle gate. As he entered the courtyard, a huge yellow lion sprang at him with a thunderous roar, but he slew it with a thrust of his sword. A gigantic black serpent as thick as a tree trunk slithered toward him, hissing. He cut off its head with a single blow. Terrifying, ghostly figures crowded around him, moaning and shrieking, but Sir Cador stalked on, paying them no heed.

Eliaures appeared. "Hold, Sir Knight," said he. "What do you seek from me?"

"I would know how the enchantment you put upon Sir Caradoc can be removed," answered Cador. "I urge you to tell me or I vow I shall slay you despite all your powers of magic!"

Eliaures felt fear grow within him, for he was not a brave man. Perhaps Cador *could* slay him in spite of all his magical powers. "I shall tell you," he said.

"Only someone who loves Caradoc more than life itself, and who is willing to take Caradoc's place can break the enchantment. That person must stand near Caradoc and call out, 'Serpent, I offer fresh food.' Then the snake will leave Caradoc and crawl, swift as a flash of lightning, to the other person. Once the snake has left Caradoc, it can be killed. But if it is not killed before it reaches the other person, that person will be doomed. Caradoc will live, but the other will become the serpent's new food and will die!"

Sir Cador left the Enchanter's castle and rode back to the castle of Sir Caradoc, where his sister waited. He told her what he had learned.

"I will take Caradoc's place!" exclaimed Guimier. "I will offer myself to the serpent. When it leaves Caradoc, you must kill it, Cador."

"But what if I cannot?" cried Cador. "The Enchanter said it will move as swiftly as a lightning flash. If I should be too slow, or if my sword misses its blow, you will be doomed! You cannot risk such a dreadful fate."

"I must," said she. "Sir Caradoc will surely die if we do not try to help him. I love him, and I will gladly risk my life to save him."

Hastily, they rode to the monastery where Caradoc lay dying. He was close to death now, but when Guimier and Cador told him what they wanted to do, he feebly shook his head.

"I would rather die than let you take such a risk, dear Guimier," he whispered. "You must not do it."

"It is the only way we can save you, Caradoc," she said, with tears in her eyes. "I *must* do it." She looked toward Sir Cador. "Have your sword ready, my brother," said she.

With a grim and worried face, Sir Cador drew his sword.

"Serpent, I offer fresh food," cried Guimier, bravely.

The snake lifted its head from Caradoc's arm and gazed at Guimier. Here, indeed, was fresh, tempting food. Caradoc was now nothing but skin and bones, but Guimier was plump and healthy. Swiftly as a bolt of lightning slashing through a stormy sky, the serpent sped down Caradoc's body and across the floor toward Guimier.

With a prayer, Cador struck. Down flashed his sword. The serpent was no more than three fingers away from Guimier's foot when the blade struck it and cut it cleanly in two!

Thus did the great bravery of the Lady Guimier rescue Sir Caradoc from the wicked enchantment. In time, Sir Caradoc grew strong and healthy again, and he and Guimier were married. And, in truth, they lived happily ever after.

A Short Dictionary of Myth and Legend

Here, in alphabetical order, are the people, places, events, and things—real and imaginary—that you have met in this book, as well as many more that you will read about in other books of myths and legends. After each entry, you'll see how to say the word: **Achilles** (uh KIHL eez). The part in capital letters is said more loudly than the rest of the word. The short description after each entry identifies the person, place, event, or thing. A **boldface** word in the description means that there is a separate entry for that word.

Achilles (uh KIHL eez) was a great hero in Greek mythology. He was killed by **Paris** in the **Trojan War.**

Adonis (uh DAHN uhs) was a handsome youth in Greek mythology. When he was killed by a wild boar, flowers sprang up from his blood.

Aegeus (EE jee uhs), a legendary king of Athens, was the father of the Greek hero **Theseus.**

Aeolus (EE uh luhs) was the god of the winds in Greek mythology.

Agamemnon (ag uh MEHM nahn) was a legendary Greek king who led the Greeks in the **Trojan War.**

Ahto (AH toh) was the lord of the sea in Finnish mythology.

Aillen (AY luhn), in Irish mythology, was a monster who came each year to burn the city of **Tara.**

Amazon (AM uh zahn) was any one of a race of women warriors in Greek legend.

Amon (AH muhn) was the chief god in ancient Egyptian mythology.

Andromeda (an DRAHM uh duh), in Greek mythology, was the daughter of King **Cepheus** and Queen **Cassiopeia.** Her life was saved by the hero **Perseus.**

Anubis (uh NOO bihs) was the god in Egyptian mythology who weighed the hearts of the dead on the scale of justice.

Aphrodite (af ruh DY tee) was the Greek goddess of love. The Romans called her **Venus.**

Apollo (uh PAHL oh) was the Greek and Roman god of the sun, poetry, music, and archery.

Arabian Nights (uh RAY bee uhn myts) is a collection of folk tales from Arabia, Egypt, India, and Persia. It has stories of Aladdin, Ali Baba, **Sinbad, and others.**

Ares (AIR eez) was the Greek god of war. The Romans called him **Mars.**

Argonaut (AHR guh nawt) was any one of the legendary Greek heroes who traveled with **Jason** in search of the **Golden Fleece.**

Argus (AHR guhs) was a giant in Greek mythology. He had a hundred eyes. When he was killed by **Hermes,** his eyes were put in the tail of the peacock.

Ariadne (ar ee AD nee) was the daughter of King **Minos.** She fell in love with **Theseus** and gave him the secret of the **Labyrinth.**

Artemis (AHR tuh mihs) was the Greek goddess of the moon and of hunting. The Romans called her **Diana.**

Arthur (AHR thuhr) was a legendary king of Britain who gathered about him the famous Knights of the Round Table.

Asgard (AS gahrd) was the home of the Norse gods and of heroes killed in battle.

Ask (ahsk), in Norse mythology, was the first man. He was created by **Odin,** along with **Embla,** the first woman.

Athena (uh THEE nuh) was the Greek goddess of war and wisdom. The Romans called her **Minerva.**

Atlas (AT luhs) was a giant, or **Titan,** in Greek mythology. He supported the world on his shoulders.

Atropos (AT ruh puhs), *see* **Fates.**

Aurora (aw RAWR uh) was the Roman goddess of the dawn. The Greeks called her **Eos.**

Baba Yaga (BAH bah YAH gah) is a death or storm **witch** who appears in Russian folklore.

Bacchus (BAK uhs) was the Roman god of wine and wild behavior. The Greeks called him **Dionysus.**

Balder (BAWL duhr) was the Norse god of light, goodness, wisdom, and peace. He was the brother of **Hoder,** the god of darkness.

banshee (BAN shee) is a fairy in Irish and Scottish folklore. Her wail is supposed to mean that there will soon be a death in the family.

basilisk (BAS uh lihsk) is a legendary reptile whose breath and look were thought to be fatal.

Beowulf (BAY uh wulf) was a legendary hero in English literature and a king of the Swedish Geats.

berserker (BUR sur kuhr) was, in ancient Norse legend, a warrior so fierce on the battlefield that he needed no armor.

bodach (BOH duhk) is a **goblin** in Irish and Scottish folklore.

boggart (BAHG uhrt) is a shy, tricky **goblin** in English folklore.

bogy (BOH gee) is a **goblin** in English folklore.

Boreas (BAWR ee uhs) was the Greek god of the north wind.

Bragi (BRAH gee), the son of **Odin** and **Frigg,** was the Norse god of poetry.

brownie (BROW nee) is a good-natured **elf** or **fairy** in English folklore.

Brunhild (BROON hihld), in German legend, was the queen of Iceland. She became the wife of King **Gunther,** for whom she was won by **Siegfried.** In Norse legend, she was a **Valkyrie** and the wife of **Gunnar,** for whom she was won by **Sigurd.** *See also Nibelungenlied; Volsunga Saga.*

bunyip (BUHN yihp) is a fabulous creature in native Australian mythology that lives at the bottom of lakes and water holes.

Cadmus (KAD muhs) was a legendary Greek prince who founded the city of Thebes and the ill-fated family that included **Oedipus.** When Cadmus killed a dragon and sowed its teeth in the ground, living soldiers sprang up.

Cador (KAY dawr) was a Knight of the Round Table.

Calliope (kuh LY uh pee), *see* **Muse.**

Camelot (KAM uh laht) was the legendary place in Britain where King **Arthur** had his court and palace.

Caradoc (KAR uh dahk) was a Knight of the Round Table.

Cassandra (kuh SAN druh) was the daughter of King **Priam.** In Greek mythology, **Apollo** gave her the power to foretell the future. Later, in anger, he punished her by ordering that no one should believe her.

Cassiopeia (kas ee uh PEE uh) was the wife of King **Cepheus** and the mother of **Andromeda** in Greek mythology.

Castor (KAS tuhr) was, in Greek mythology, one of the twin sons of **Zeus** by **Leda.** Castor was mortal. His twin, **Pollux,** was immortal.

Centaur (SEHN tawr) was a creature in Greek mythology who was half man and half horse.

Cepheus (SEE fee uhs) was a king in Greek mythology. He was the husband of **Cassiopeia** and the father of **Andromeda.**

Cerberus (SUR buhr uhs) was the three-headed dog in Greek and Roman mythology who guarded the gate to **Hades.**

Ceres (SIHR eez) was the Roman goddess of agriculture. The Greeks called her **Demeter.**

Charon (KAIR uhn) was the boatman in Greek mythology who took the souls of the dead across the River **Styx.**

Chimera (kuh MIHR uh) was a fire-breathing monster in Greek mythology. It had the head of a lion, the body of a goat, and the tail of a serpent.

Circe (SUR see) was a beautiful woman in Greek mythology who had the power to change men into beasts.

Clio (KLY oh), *see* **Muse.**

Clotho (KLOH thoh), *see* **Fates.**

Clytemnestra (kly tuhm NEHS truh) was the wife of **Agamemnon** in Greek legend. She murdered him upon his return from the **Trojan War.** In turn, she was murdered by her son, **Orestes.**

Coyote (KY oht *or* ky OH tee) is a cunning figure, human or animal, in the myths of many North American Indian tribes.

Cronus (KROH nuhs) was the son of **Uranus** and the father of **Zeus** in Greek mythology. He was the ruler of the **Titans** until overthrown by Zeus. The Romans identified him with **Saturn.**

Cuchulain (koo HUHL ihn) was a great warrior and hero in Irish legends.

Cupid (KYOO pihd) was the Roman god of love. The Greeks called him **Eros.**

Cyclops (SY klahps) was one of a group of giants in Greek mythology. Each had a single eye in the center of his forehead.

Daedalus (DEHD uh luhs) was an architect in Greek mythology and the builder of the **Labyrinth.** He and his son **Icarus** were imprisoned there, but escaped by making wings with which to fly.

Daphne (DAF nee) was a **nymph** in Greek mythology. She was saved from the attentions of **Apollo** by being turned into a laurel tree.

Dasharatha (DASH uh huh rah) was the king of the night sky in Hindu mythology and the father of the great hero, **Rama.**

Deimos (DY mahs) was the son of **Ares** and the Greek demigod of terror.

Deirdre (DIHR dree) was a heroine in ancient Irish legends. Her love for a nephew of the king set off wars and tragedy.

Demeter (dih MEE tuhr) was the Greek goddess of agriculture. The Romans called her **Ceres.**

Diana (dy AN uh) was the Roman goddess of the moon and of hunting. The Greeks called her **Artemis.**

Dionysus (dy uh NY suhs) was the Greek god of wine and wild behavior. The Romans called him **Bacchus.**

dragon (DRAG uhn) is a mythical beast in the folklore of many European and Asian cultures. In Europe, a dragon is usually a huge, fierce beast with wings, claws, and a long, scaly tail. It often breathes fire and smoke. But in Asia, especially in China and Japan, dragons are generally considered friendly creatures that bring good luck and wealth.

dryad (DRY uhd) was a wood **nymph** in Greek mythology. Dryads lived in trees and died when their tree died.

dwarf (dwawrf) is a small, often ugly little man with magic powers. Dwarfs appear in many folk tales.

Echidna (ih KIHD nuh) was a monster in Greek mythology who gave birth to **Cerberus,** the **Chimera,** and the **Sphinx.**

Echo (EHK oh) was a **nymph** in Greek mythology who pined away with love for **Narcissus** until nothing was left but her voice.

Electra (ih LEHK truh) was a tragic heroine in Greek legend. She helped her brother, **Orestes,** kill their mother, **Clytemnestra,** to avenge the murder of their father, **Agamemnon.**

elf (ehlf) is a tiny person that appears in northern European folklore. Elves have magical powers. They can do good deeds or cause misfortune.

Eliaures (ee lih AU rees) was an enchanter in legends of King **Arthur.**

Embla (EHM bluh), in Norse mythology, was the first woman. She was created by **Odin,** along with **Ask,** the first man.

Eos (EE ahs) was the Greek goddess of the dawn. The Romans called her **Aurora.**

Epimetheus (ehp uh MEE thoos), in Greek mythology, was the brother of **Prometheus** and husband of **Pandora.**

Erato (EHR uh toh), *see* **Muse.**

Eris (IHR ihs) was the Greek goddess of strife and discord.

Erlking (URL kihng) is a legendary German **goblin** that does harm, especially to children.

Eros (IHR ahs) was the Greek god of love and son of **Aphrodite.** The Romans called him **Cupid.**

Europa (yoo ROH puh) was a beautiful maiden in Greek mythology who was loved by **Zeus.** He took the form of a white bull and carried her off to Crete. Europa was the mother of King **Minos.**

Eurydice (yoo RIHD uh see) was, in Greek mythology, the wife of **Orpheus.** He freed her from **Hades** by the charm of his music, but lost her again because he disobeyed instructions and turned around to see if she were following him.

Eurystheus (yoo RIHS thoos *or* yoo RIHS thee uhs), in Greek mythology, was the king who commanded **Hercules** to perform the twelve labors.

Euterpe (yoo TUR pee), *see* **Muse.**

Excalibur (ehk SKAL uh buhr) was the magic sword **Arthur** drew from a stone to prove he was the king.

Fafnir (FAHV nihr), in Norse mythology, was the dragon that guarded the **Nibelungs'** treasure until slain by **Sigurd.**

fairy (FAIR ee) is a supernatural being with magic powers. Fairies appear in the folklore of many cultures and can do both good and harm.

Fates (fayts) were the three goddesses in Greek and Roman mythology who controlled the lives of humans. They were Clotho (KLOH thoh), who spun the thread of life; Lachesis (LAK uh sihs), who decided how long it should be; and Atropos (AT ruh puhs), who cut it off.

Faunus (FAW nuhs), *see* **Pan.**

Fenrir (FEHN rihr), in Norse mythology, was the wolflike monster that killed **Odin.**

fetish (FEHT ihsh), in many African mythologies, is a temporary home on earth for a divinity.

Fiana (FEE uh nuh) was a group of warriors famous in Irish legend.

Finn MacCool (fihn MAK kool) was a legendary Irish hero and leader of the **Fiana.**

Flora (FLAWR uh) was the Roman goddess of flowers.

Fortuna (fawr TOO nuh) was the Roman goddess of chance, luck, or fortune.

Frey (fray) was the Norse god of love, peace, and plenty.

Freya (FRAY uh) was the Norse goddess of love and beauty.

Frigg (frihg) was the wife of **Odin** and the Norse goddess of love and the sky.

Furies (FYUR eez) were the three terrible goddesses of vengeance in Greek and Roman mythology. They pursued those guilty of sin and drove them mad.

Galahad (GAL uh had) was the noblest of the Knights of the Round Table.

Ganymede (GAN uh meed) was a beautiful youth in Greek mythology who became cupbearer to the gods.

Gareth (GAR uhth) was a Knight of the Round Table and nephew of King **Arthur.**

Gawain (GAH wihn) was a Knight of the Round Table.

Geb (gehb) was the ancient Egyptian god of the earth.

George (jawrj) is the patron saint of England. Although a real person, his life is surrounded by legend, such as the story about his killing a **dragon.**

ghoul (gool) is a horrible demon in Oriental stories.

giant (JY uhnt) is an imaginary being like a man, but much larger and stronger. Giants appear in the folklore of many cultures.

Gilgamesh (GIHL guh mehsh) was a legendary Babylonian king and the hero of the *Epic of Gilgamesh.*

Glooscap (GLUS kap) is a super being who appears in many of the legends of the Micmac Indians of eastern Canada.

gnome (nohm) is a **dwarf** in Norse folklore.

goblin (GAHB luhn) is an ugly looking, evil **dwarf** that appears in the folklore of many cultures.

Golden Fleece (GOHL duhn flees) was a ram's coat made of gold and guarded by a dragon. In Greek legend, **Jason** and the **Argonauts** searched for and finally took it.

Gorgon (GAWR guhn) was any one of three sisters in Greek mythology who had snakes for hair and faces so horrible that anyone who looked at them turned to stone. *See also* **Medusa.**

Graces (GRAY sihz) were three sister goddesses in Greek and Roman mythology who gave beauty, charm, and joy to people and nature.

Green Knight (green nyt) was the huge man, all in green, who challenged Sir **Gawain** to chop off his head.

Grendel (GREHN duhl) was a monster killed by **Beowulf.**

griffin (GRIHF uhn) is a mythical animal with the head, wings, and forelegs of an eagle, and the body, hind legs, and tail of a lion.

Guinevere (GWIHN uh vihr) was the queen of King **Arthur.**

Gunnar (GUN ahr) is a king in the Icelandic legend, the *Volsunga Saga.* In the German version of this tale, his name is **Gunther.**

Gunther (GUN tuhr) is a legendary king in the German epic poem, the *Nibelungenlied.* In the Icelandic version of the tale, his name is **Gunnar.**

Hades (HAY deez) was the god of the dead in Greek mythology. He ruled the kingdom of the dead, which was also called Hades. The Roman name for this god was **Pluto.**

Hanuman (HAN yoo man) was the monkey general who aided **Rama** in the great work of Hindu literature, the *Ramayana.*

Harpy (HAHR pee) was a winged monster, part woman and part bird, in Greek and Roman mythology. They were three sisters, who lived in filth and took the souls of the dead.

Hebe (HEE bee) was the Greek goddess of youth and spring.

Hecate (HEHK uh tee) was the Greek goddess of the moon and earth.

Hector (HEHK tuhr), a hero in Greek legend, was the bravest of all the Trojans in the **Trojan War.**

Hel (hehl) was the daughter of **Loki** and the Norse goddess of death. Hel is also the home of Norse warriors not slain in battle.

Helen (HEHL uhn), in Greek legend, was the most beautiful of all women. She was married to King **Menelaus. Paris** took her to **Troy,** and this is what caused the **Trojan War.**

Helios (HEE lee ahs) was the Greek god of the sun.

Hephaestus (hih FEHS tuhs) was the Greek god of fire and metalworking. The Romans called him **Vulcan.**

Hera (HIHR uh), the wife of **Zeus** in Greek mythology, was the queen of

the gods and the goddess of women
and marriage. The Romans called her
Juno.

Heracles, *see* **Hercules.**

Hercules (HUR kyuh leez), called
Heracles (HEHR uh kleez) by the
Greeks, was a son of **Zeus** and a hero
in Greek and Roman myths. He was
noted for his great strength. Hercules
was commanded by King **Eurystheus**
to perform twelve great labors, after
which he would become immortal.

Hermes (HUR meez) was the messenger
of the gods in Greek mythology. The
Romans called him **Mercury.**

Hippolyta (hih PAHL uh tuh) was a
queen of the **Amazons** in Greek
legend.

Hoder (HOH dur) was the Norse god of
darkness and brother of **Balder,** the
god of light.

Holy Grail (HOH lee grayl) was the cup
supposed to have been used by Christ
at the Last Supper. It was an object
of search by the Knights of the
Round Table.

Homer (HOH muhr) is traditionally
considered the blind Greek poet who
wrote the great epics, the *Iliad* and
the *Odyssey.*

Horus (HAWR uhs) was a sun god of
ancient Egypt. He is usually shown as
having the head of a hawk.

Hydra (HY druh) was a monster in
Greek mythology that had nine heads.
It was killed by **Hercules.**

Icarus (IHK uhr uhs), in Greek legend,
the son of **Daedalus,** who built wings
of wax and feathers so that they could
escape from prison. When Icarus flew
too close to the sun, the wax melted.
Icarus fell into the sea and drowned.

Iku-Turso (Y koo TUR soh) is an evil
water spirit in the Finnish epic, the
Kalevala.

Iliad (IHL ee uhd) is a long Greek epic
poem, supposedly by **Homer,** that
describes the **Trojan War.**

Ilmarinen (ihl mahr IHN ehn) was a
skilled smith and one of the heroes in
the Finnish epic, the *Kalevala.*

Iris (Y rihs) was the Greek goddess of
the rainbow.

Isis (Y sihs) was the chief goddess of
ancient Egypt and the wife of **Osiris.**

Janet (JAN eht) is the heroine of an old
Scottish ballad who saves **Tam Lin**
from the fairies.

Janus (JAY nuhs) was the Roman god
of doors and of beginnings and
endings. Janus had two faces, one
looking forward and one looking
backward.

Jason (JAY suhn) was the Greek hero
who led the search for the **Golden
Fleece.**

Jatayu (jay TAY yoo) is the eagle king
in the Hindu epic, the *Ramayana,*
who dies trying to save **Sita.**

jinni (jih NEE), or **djinni,** is a spirit in
Muslim mythology that can appear in
human or animal form. A jinni can do
both good and evil. The plural is jinn.

Juno (JOO noh) was the wife of **Jupiter**
in Roman mythology. The Greeks
called her **Hera.**

Jupiter (JOO puh tuhr) was the ruler of
the gods in Roman mythology. The
Greeks called him **Zeus.**

Kalevala (KAH lai val lah) is the
national epic of Finland. It consists of
centuries-old song-poems and chants
collected by Elias Lönnrot, a country
doctor. The work tells of the
adventures of three heroes—
Ilmarinen, Lemminkainen, and
Vainamoinen—and their raids
against **Louhi,** the queen of Pohjola.

Kay (kay) was a Knight of the Round
Table.

kelpie (KEHL pee) is a water spirit in
Scottish folklore. It takes the form of
a horse, and is supposed to drown
people or warn them of drowning.

kobold (KOH bahld) is a **goblin** in German folklore. Some kobolds do household work; others haunt mines and caves.

Kullervo (kuhl EHR voh) was a magician in the Finnish epic, the *Kalevala.*

Labyrinth (LAB uh rihnth), in Greek mythology, was the maze built by **Daedalus** in which King **Minos** imprisoned the **Minotaur.**

Lachesis (LAK uh sihs), *see* **Fates.**

Lakshmana (LAHKSH mahna) was the younger brother of **Rama** in the Hindu epic, the *Ramayana.*

Lancelot (LAN suh luht) was the bravest of the Knights of the Round Table.

Lanka (LAHNG kuh) was the home of the evil **Rakshas** in the Hindu epic, the *Ramayana.*

Laocoon (lay AHK oh ahn) was the priest in the **Trojan War** who warned the Trojans against the wooden horse that the Greeks used to capture **Troy.**

Leda (LEE duh) was a queen in Greek mythology. **Zeus** came to her in the form of a swan and she gave birth to twin sons, **Castor** and **Pollux.**

Lemminkainen (lehm ihn KAY nihn) was one of the heroes in the Finnish epic, the *Kalevala.*

leprechaun (LEHP ruh kawn), in Irish legends, is an **elf** who looks like a little old man. Leprechauns are said to have hidden gold and can be made to reveal the hiding place if they are caught.

Loki (loh kee) was the Norse god of destruction and the brother of **Odin.**

Louhi (LOO ee) was the queen of Pohjola in the Finnish epic, the *Kalevala.* She personifies the forces of darkness and cold.

Mab (mab) was the queen of the fairies in English folklore.

Manitou (MAN uh toh) was the Great Spirit of the Algonkian Indians of North America. The Gitche-Manito was a good spirit. The Matche-Manito was an evil spirit.

manticore (MAN tih kawr) was a fabulous, legendary monster having the head of a man, the body of a lion, and the tail or sting of a scorpion.

Mars (mahrs) was the Roman god of war. The Greeks called him **Ares.**

Martha (MAR thuh) was a Christian saint who is said to have captured the **Tarasque** with only holy water and courage.

Medea (mih DEE uh) was an enchantress in Greek mythology who helped **Jason** win the **Golden Fleece.**

Medusa (muh DOO suh) was one of the three **Gorgons** in Greek mythology.

Melpomene (mehl PAHM uh nee), *see* **Muse.**

Menelaus (mehn uh LAY uhs) was a king of Sparta in Greek legend. He was the brother of **Agamemnon,** and the husband of **Helen.**

Mercury (MUR kyuhr ee) was the messenger of the gods in Roman mythology. The Greeks called him **Hermes.**

Merlin (MER luhn) was a powerful magician who instructed King **Arthur.**

Midas (MY duhs) was a king in Greek mythology who was given the power to turn everything he touched into gold.

Mimir (MEE mihr) was the giant who guarded the spring of wisdom in Norse mythology.

Minerva (muh NER vuh) was the Roman goddess of war and wisdom. The Greeks called her **Athena.**

Minos (MY nuhs) was the king of Crete who had the **Labyrinth** built for the **Minotaur.**

Minotaur (MIHN uh tawr) was a monster in Greek legend who had the body of a man and the head of a bull.

Kept in the **Labyrinth** of King **Minos,** it was killed by **Theseus.**

Mnemosyne (ni MAHS uh nee) was the Greek goddess of memory and mother of the **Muses.**

Modred (MOH drehd) was a Knight of the Round Table.

Molloch, May (MOH lahk, may) is an **elf** in Irish and Scottish folklore who takes part in sports.

Momotaro (moh moh TAHR oh) is the hero of a popular Japanese legend. He is also known as the Peach Boy.

Momus (MOH muhs) was the Greek god of ridicule. He was thrown out of heaven for his sharp tongue.

Morgan le Fey (MAWR guhn luh FAY) was a scheming, evil fairy and the half sister of King **Arthur.**

Muse (myooz) was any one of the nine goddesses of the arts and sciences in Greek mythology. They were the daughters of **Zeus** and **Mnemosyne,** and served as a source of inspiration for writers and artists. Each Muse ruled over a certain art or science. Calliope (kuh LY uh pee) was the Muse of epic poetry; Clio (KLY oh), history; Erato (EHR uh toh), love poetry; Euterpe (yoo TUR pee), lyric poetry; Melpomene (mehl PAHM uh nee), tragedy; Polyhymnia (pahl ee HIHM nee uh), sacred song; Terpsichore (turp SIHK uh ree), dance; Thalia (thuh LY uh), comedy; and Urania (yu RAY nee uh), astronomy.

naid (NAY ad) is any one of a number of beautiful young nymphs who guard and give life to streams and springs in Greek mythology.

Nanna (NAHN nuh) was the wife of **Balder** in Norse mythology. Grieving for his death, she threw herself into the flames of his funeral pyre.

Narcissus (nahr SIHS uhs) was a handsome youth in Greek mythology. He fell in love with his own reflection in a pool of water and pined away

until all that was left was the flower called a narcissus.

Nemesis (NEHM uh sihs) was the Greek goddess of vengeance.

Neptune (NEHP toon) was the Roman god of the sea. The Greeks called him **Poseidon.**

Nereid (NIHR ee ihd) was any of the fifty sea nymphs who attended the sea god **Poseidon** (**Neptune**).

Nibelung (NEE buh lung) was any one of a group of northern **dwarfs** in German legend who had a hoard of gold and a magic ring. Also any of the followers of **Siegfried** who captured the gold and the magic ring.

Nibelungenlied (NEE buh lung uhn leet) is a German epic poem that tells of the adventures of **Siegfried.** The title means "Song of the Nibelungs." *See also **Volsunga Saga.***

nixie (NIHK see) is a female water **fairy** in German legend.

Norn (nawn) was any one of the three Norse goddesses of fate: Urd (past), Verdande (present), and Skuld (future).

Nox (nahks) was the Roman goddess of night. The Greeks called her **Nyx.**

Nyame (ny AHM ee) was, among the Ashanti of Africa, the creator of the universe.

nymph (nihmf) was, among Greeks and Romans, a lesser goddess of nature.

Nyx (nihks) was the Greek goddess of night. The Romans called her **Nox.**

Oberon (OH buh rahn) was the king of the fairies in English folklore.

Oceanus (oh SEE uh nuhs) was the Greek god of the stream that was supposed to surround all land.

Odin (OH dihn) was the chief god in Norse mythology.

Odysseus (oh DIHS ee uhs *or* oh DIHS yoos) was a hero in Greek legend and the main character in the *Odyssey.* The Romans called him Ulysses (yoo LIHS eez). *See also* **Penelope.**

Odyssey (AHD uh see) is a Greek epic poem, supposedly written by the blind poet **Homer.** It tells of the adventures of **Odysseus** during his ten years of wandering after the **Trojan War.** *See also* **Penelope.**

ogre (OH guhr) is a hideous giant in many folklores that is supposed to eat people.

Olympus (oh LIHM puhs) is the highest mountain in Greece. The early Greeks believed that it was the home of the gods.

Orestes (aw REHS teez) was a tragic character in Greek mythology. Orestes killed his mother, **Clytemnestra,** to avenge the murder of his father, **Agamemnon.** He was pursued by the **Furies** for his crime.

Orion (aw RY uhn) was a giant hunter of great strength in Greek mythology. A son of **Poseidon,** he was accidentally killed by **Artemis.**

Orpheus (AWR fee uhs) was a musician in Greek mythology. He played his lyre so beautifully that animals, trees, and even rocks followed him. *See also* **Eurydice.**

Osiris (oh SY rihs) was one of the chief gods of ancient Egypt. He was the ruler of the lower world and judge of the dead.

Ossian (AHSH ee an) was a legendary Irish warrior and the son of **Finn MacCool.**

Pan (pan) was the Greek god of forests, pastures, flocks, and shepherds. He is described as a man with the legs, horns, and ears of a goat who wandered through the woods and fields playing music on his pipes. The Romans called him Faunus (FAW nuhs).

Pandora (pan DAWR uh), in Greek mythology, was the first woman. Curiosity led her to open a box and so let out all sorts of troubles into the world.

Paris (PAR ihs) was the son of **Priam.** He took **Helen** to **Troy,** and so started the **Trojan War.**

Pegasus (PEHG uh suhs) was a winged horse in Greek mythology.

Penelope (puh NEHL uh pee) was the faithful wife of **Odysseus** in Greek legend. Despite many suitors, she waited twenty years for his return.

Persephone (puhr SEHF uh nee), in Greek mythology, was carried off to the Underworld by **Hades,** who made her his queen. She was allowed to spend only part of each year on earth. The Romans called her **Proserpina.**

Perseus (PER see uhs) was a hero in Greek mythology. He slew **Medusa** and rescued **Andromeda** from a sea monster.

Phaethon (FAY uh thahn) was the son of **Helios.** One day he tried to drive the sun, his father's chariot. He nearly set fire to the earth, so **Zeus** struck him down with a thunderbolt.

Phoenix (FEE nihks) is a mythical bird that, according to Greek legend, rises from its own ashes to live again.

pixy or **pixie** (PIHK see) is a cheerful **elf** in the folklore of Cornwall and Devon, England. Also called "piskeys," these elves like to play tricks on people.

Pluto (PLOO toh) was the Roman god of the dead. The Greeks called him **Hades.**

Pollux (PAHL uhks) was an immortal son of **Leda** by **Zeus.** His twin, **Castor** was mortal.

Polyhymnia (pahl ee HIHM nee uh), *see* **Muse.**

Poseidon (puh SY duhn) was the Greek god of the sea and of horses. The Romans called him **Neptune.**

Priam (PRY uhm), in Greek mythology, was the king of **Troy** at the time of the **Trojan War.**

Prometheus (pruh MEE thee uhs) was a **Titan** in Greek mythology who stole fire from the gods and taught men to use it.

Proserpina (proh SUR puh nuh), *see* **Persephone.**

Psyche (SY kee), in Greek and Roman mythology, was a beautiful young girl who was loved by **Eros** and made immortal by **Zeus.**

Ra (rah) or **Re** (ray) was the ancient Egyptian god of the sun.

Rakshas (RAHK shas) were the demon people of **Lanka** in the *Ramayana.*

Rama (RAH muh) was the hero of the Hindu epic, the *Ramayana.*

Ramayana (rah MAH yuh nuh), or "Romance of Rama," is a great epic poem of India and of Hindu mythology.

Ran (rahn) was a Norse sea goddess who caught drowning men in her nets.

Ravana (rah VAH nuh) was the king of the demon **Rakshas** in the great Hindu epic, the *Ramayana.*

Remus (REE muhs), in Roman mythology, was the twin brother of **Romulus.** He was killed by Romulus for leaping over the walls of Rome.

roc (rahk) was a huge, legendary bird, so strong it could carry off an elephant. It figures in the tales of **Sinbad** in the *Arabian Nights.*

Romulus (RAHM yuh luhs) was the legendary founder and first king of Rome. He and his twin brother **Remus,** abandoned as infants, were found and nourished by a wolf.

Sampo (SAM poh) is a magical object in the Finnish epic, the *Kalevala.* It is often pictured as a three-sided mill that grinds out grain, salt, and gold.

Saturn (SAT uhrn) was an early god in Roman mythology. The Romans identified him with the Greek god **Cronus.**

satyr (SAT uhr) was a Greek deity of the woods, part man and part goat.

Set (seht) was the ancient Egyptian god of evil.

Siegfried (SEEG freed) was a great hero in German legends. He killed a dragon, won the treasure of the **Nibelungs,** and won **Brunhild** for King **Gunther.**

Sigurd (SIHG urd) was a great hero in Norse legends. He is identified with the German hero, **Siegfried.**

Sinbad (SIHN bad) was a sailor in the *Arabian Nights* who had seven fantastic voyages.

Siren (SY ruhn) was any one of a group of **nymphs** in Greek and Roman mythology. Their sweet singing lured sailors to destruction on the rocks.

Sita (SEE tah) was the wife of **Rama** and the heroine of the Hindu epic, the *Ramayana.*

Sphinx (sfihngks) is an imaginary creature in many ancient myths. In Greek mythology, it was a monster with the head of a woman, the body of a lion, and wings. The Sphinx asked a riddle and killed anyone unable to guess the answer. An Egyptian sphinx (such as the Great Sphinx) had the head of a man and the body of a lion.

Styx (stihks) is a river in Greek and Roman mythology that surrounds **Hades.** The boatman **Charon** carried the souls of the dead across this river. The gods took their most sacred oaths by the name of the River Styx.

Sugriva (soo GREE vuh) was the monkey king who helped **Rama** in the Hindu epic, the *Ramayana.*

Sumangaru (soo MAN guh ruh) was the last ruler of what was once the great Ghana Empire in Africa. A real person, he is depicted as a sorcerer in legends about **Sundiata.**

Sundiata (suhn dee AH tah) was a real person who ruled the Mali Empire in West Africa. The Malinke people have many legends about his great deeds.

Tam Lin (tam lihn) is the hero of an old Scottish ballad. He was saved from the fairies by **Janet.**

Tara (TAR uh), a low hill in Ireland, is famous in legend and history as the home of the early Irish kings.

Tarasque (tar ASK) was the dragon captured by Saint **Martha.**

Terpsichore (turp SIHK uh ree), *see* **Muse.**

Theseus (THEE see uhs *or* THEE soos) was the hero in Greek mythology who killed the **Minotaur.**

Thor (thawr) was the Norse god of thunder and lightning. He had a magic hammer, made by **dwarfs,** that never missed its mark and always returned to him.

Titan (TY tuhn), in Greek mythology, was one of a family of giants who ruled the world before the gods of Mount **Olympus.**

Tristram (TRIHS truhm) was one of the most famous of the Knights of the Round Table.

Triton (TRY tuhn) was a sea god in Greek mythology. He had the head and body of a man and the tail of a fish.

Trojan War (TROH juhn wawr) was a war between Greece and the city of **Troy.** It took place more than three thousand years ago and lasted for ten years before Troy was defeated. *See also* **Achilles, Agamemnon, Clytemnestra, Hector, Helen, Homer,** *Iliad,* **Menelaus, Paris, Priam.**

troll (trohl) is an ugly **dwarf** or **giant** in Norse mythology. In most folk tales, they are huge **ogres.**

Troy (troy), also called Ilium (IHL ee uhm), was an ancient city in Asia Minor that was made famous in legends of early Greece. The Greeks attacked and destroyed it more than three thousand years ago in the **Trojan War.** *See also* **Achilles, Agamemnon, Clytemnestra, Hector, Helen, Homer,** *Iliad,* **Menelaus, Paris, Priam.**

Tugarin (too GAR ihn) is a dragon that appears in Russian folklore.

Ulysses (yoo LIHS eez), *see* **Odysseus.**

Ukko (YOO koh) is the Lord of the Sky called upon by **Louhi** in the *Kalevala.*

unicorn (YOO nuh kawrn) is an imaginary animal like a horse but with a single, long, spiral horn in the middle of its forehead and the tail of a lion.

Urania (yu RAY nee uh), *see* **Muse.**

Uranus (yu RAY nuhs) was the earliest god of the sky in Greek and Roman mythology and the father of the **Titans.**

Uutar (YOO tahr) is the Spirit of Fogs called upon by **Louhi** in the *Kalevala.*

Vainamoinen (vahn ah MOYN uhn) is a powerful magician and one of the heroes of the *Kalevala.*

Valhalla (val HAL uh), in Norse mythology, was the hall in **Asgard** where heroes slain in battle feasted with **Odin.**

Valkyrie (val KIHR ee) was, in Norse mythology, any one of the twelve handmaidens of **Odin.** The Valkyries watched over battlefields, chose the heroes who were to die, and led them to **Valhalla.**

Venus (VEE nuhs) was the Roman goddess of love and beauty. Cupid was her son. The Greeks called her **Aphrodite.**

Vetahinen (veht ah HY nuhn) is an evil water spirit in the Finnish epic, the *Kalevala.*

Vishnu (VIHSH noo) is the supreme spirit of Hindu religion. In one of his nine reincarnations, Vishnu appeared as **Rama,** the hero of the Hindu epic, the *Ramayana.*

Volsung (VAHL sung) was a powerful king in Norse mythology and one of the heroes of the *Volsunga Saga.*

Volsunga Saga (VAHL sung guh SAH guh) is an Icelandic prose legend that tells of the adventures of **Sigurd.** The

title means "Saga of the Volsungs."
See also **Nibelungenlied.**

Vulcan (VUHL kuhn) was the Roman god of fire and metalworking. The Greeks called him **Hephaestus.**

Wiglaf (WIHG laf) was the brave companion who helped **Beowulf** kill a dragon. He became king of the Swedish Geats when Beowulf died.

witch (wihch) is a woman who is supposed to have magic powers. Witches appear in the folklore of many cultures and are generally considered to be evil.

wizard (WIHZ uhrd) is a man who is supposed to have magic powers. Wizards appear in the folklore of many cultures.

Wotan (WOH tuhn) was the supreme god in ancient German mythology. He is identified with **Odin.**

Ymir (EE mihr), in Norse mythology, was a giant, formed from blocks of ice and sparks of fire, from whose body the gods made the world.

Zephyrus (ZEHF uhr uhs) was the Greek god of the west wind.

Zeus (zoos), in Greek mythology, was the ruler of the gods. The Romans called him **Jupiter.**

Illustration Acknowledgments

The publishers of *Childcraft* gratefully acknowledge the courtesy of the following individuals, agencies, and organizations for illustrations in this volume. When all the illustrations for a sequence of pages are from a single source, the inclusive page numbers are given. Credits should be read from left to right, top to bottom, on their respective pages. All illustrations are the exclusive property of the publishers of *Childcraft* unless names are marked with an asterisk (*).

Cover:	Aristocrat and Standard binding—David Wenzel
	Heritage binding—Jerry Pinkney;
	David Wenzel; Katherine Coville; Yoshi
	Miyake, David Wenzel; David Wenzel;
	David Wenzel; Bert Dodson; Bert Dodson
1–3:	Yoshi Miyake
8–9:	David Wenzel; Carolyn Croll
10:	Carolyn Croll
11–18:	David Wenzel
20–21:	Allen Davis; Carolyn Croll
22:	Carolyn Croll
23–31:	Allen Davis
32–33:	Jerry Pinkney; Carolyn Croll
34:	Carolyn Croll
35–42:	Jerry Pinkney
44–45:	Doug Jamieson; Carolyn Croll
46:	Carolyn Croll
47–49:	Doug Jamieson
50–51:	Yoshi Miyake; Carolyn Croll
52:	Carolyn Croll
53–71:	Yoshi Miyake
72–73:	Pollyanna Quasthoff; Carolyn Croll
74:	Carolyn Croll
75–80:	Pollyanna Quasthoff
82–83:	Katherine Coville; Carolyn Croll
84:	Carolyn Croll
85–103:	Katherine Coville
104–105:	Troy Howell; Carolyn Croll
106:	Carolyn Croll
107–115:	Troy Howell
116–117:	Jerry Pinkney; Carolyn Croll
118:	Carolyn Croll
119–127:	Jerry Pinkney
128–129:	Michael Eagle; Carolyn Croll
130:	Carolyn Croll
131–147:	Michael Eagle
148–149:	Bert Dodson: Carolyn Croll
150:	Carolyn Croll
151–159:	Bert Dodson
160–161:	Martin Giese; Carolyn Croll
162:	Carolyn Croll
163–175:	Martin Giese
176–177:	Nancy Munger; Carolyn Croll
178:	Carolyn Croll
179–189:	Nancy Munger
190–191:	Pollyanna Quasthoff; Carolyn Croll
192:	Carolyn Croll
193–203:	Pollyanna Quasthoff
204–205:	Bert Dodson; Carolyn Croll
206:	Carolyn Croll
207–217:	Bert Dodson
218–219:	Doug Jamieson; Carolyn Croll
220:	Carolyn Croll
221–234:	Doug Jamieson
236–237:	Yoshi Miyake; Carolyn Croll
238:	Carolyn Croll
239–247:	Yoshi Miyake
248–249:	Allen Davis; Carolyn Croll
250:	Carolyn Croll
251–255:	Allen Davis
256–257:	David Wenzel; Carolyn Croll
258:	Carolyn Croll
259–279:	David Wenzel
280–281:	Michael Eagle; Carolyn Croll
282:	Carolyn Croll
283–291:	Michael Eagle